The Literary Agent's Guide to Writing a Non-Fiction Book Proposal

By Andy Ross

First published as a Kindle e-book 2016

Paperback edition through
waynegoodmanbooks

ISBN: 978-0-9888143-8-7

20180328

To Leslie with all my love

THE LITERARY AGENT'S GUIDE TO

Table of Contents

THE LITERARY AGENT'S GUIDE TO

"Book publishing is the marriage of art and commerce."

What is a Book Proposal?

To get your non-fiction book acquired by a commercial publisher, you are going to have to write a book proposal. A lot of publishing gurus and freelance editors will tell you what a daunting challenge it is to construct a proposal. My advice: don't get intimidated. Writing a great proposal isn't that difficult, at least if you have a great idea for a book. And the process of creating the proposal can help you refine your original conception and make it more appealing to an agent, a publisher, and to your readers.

This book will guide you through the process. I will lay out the essential information you need to construct a proposal that addresses the questions agents and acquisition editors will be asking and helps you to present your most compelling case for publication. I'll be using examples from real book proposals written by my clients to show the challenges these writers faced and how we dealt with those challenges.

There are many articles in periodicals like *Writers Digest* offering helpful "tips" for writing proposals. Some of them will tell you anyone can get a book published if you just follow a few simple rules. Don't believe that for a minute. I'm a realist. I've been a literary agent since 2008. I've worked on hundreds of book proposals and sent out thousands of submissions. I can tell you from experience it isn't easy getting your book published, even for a worthy project, even if you have an outstanding book proposal. This book won't provide you with any kind of secret formula or alchemical knowledge. But my advice will be honest and will lay out the issues you will have to address in every step of the process.

There's the old cliché that book publishing is the marriage of art and commerce. That's true. But right now the marriage is a little kinky. It's kind of an S/M arrangement with the commerce part holding the whip. The largest commercial publishers: Penguin-Random House, HarperCollins, Simon & Schuster, Hachette, and MacMillan are owned by international multi-media conglomerates. There may have been a time when publishing was a gentleman's pastime, a cottage industry where deals were decided between friends at the legendary three martini publisher's lunch. Those days are gone. Book publishing is a business, and the parent corporations put a huge amount of pressure on publishers to make a profit on every book they produce. In spite of this, most books still lose money and are subsidized by the big best sellers. So in this environment the writer has to think like a business person as well as an artist.

And in that spirit, a book proposal is a business plan, plain and simple. It's a highly structured document laying out what the book is, what is its relevance, who the audience is, why you are the best one to write about it, and what you will do to promote the book once it is published. Finally, not to put too fine a point on it, the proposal has to convince the publisher that your book will make money. Still, it's important to remember acquisition editors are book lovers, just like you and me. Sure. The first question they will be asking themselves is how will the book sell. But at the same time you need to inspire them, to seduce them, to make them excited about the project, to make them fall in love.

You can sell a non-fiction book project based on a proposal and a sample chapter. You don't have to write the entire book, and I strongly advise against it. The one exception to this is memoir. Some memoirs can be sold with a proposal. But others are more like novels in that the book will be evaluated on the basis of the story, the style, the voice, and whether it has a compelling narrative arc. For these books, publishers will likely insist on the finished manuscript. But even if you have completed the text of your memoir, you should still submit a proposal that will make a strong case for publishing the book. In all likelihood, the editor will be showing the proposal around the office and making a presentation at the weekly acquisition meeting. You need to provide the editor with the ammunition he needs to convince the publisher, the editor-in-chief, the marketing director, and the sales director that this is a worthy project.

When I say proposals are highly structured documents, I mean they usually employ the same standard organizational scheme. Almost all proposals include ten sections. They are: (1) the Title Page, (2) the Proposal Table of Contents, (3) The Overview, (4) Production Details, (5) The Audience, (6) The Competitive Analysis, (7) Marketing and Promotion, (8) About the

Author, (9) Table of Contents and Chapter Outline, and (10) Sample Chapter (or two). A proposal might also have an appendix with additional information. A scholar would want to provide his curriculum vitae in the appendix. A photographer would include some sample photographs. Sometimes you might use a collection of news clippings. Within this structure there is room for creativity and even a little fun. But I wouldn't deviate too much from the format. Editors are used to it and find it easier to analyze the project when it is organized in a familiar style and structure.

A bad book proposal can kill a deal for a good book. Well, maybe if you're Kim Kardashian, you can get away with a lousy proposal or none at all. But, if I may be so blunt: you, gentle reader, are not Kim Kardashian. So you will need to sell your book the old fashion way, by making an honest and convincing argument about the worth of your project.

First Steps to Getting Published

The Query Letter

Before your proposal gets to the desk of the acquisition editor, you are going to have to find an agent. The legendary publisher, Alfred Knopf, once said: "An agent is to a publisher as a knife is to a throat." Those days are gone, and now agents have an essential role in the publishing process. We have become the gate keepers of book publishing. We filter out the bad stuff, and only deliver the best quality projects for publishers to evaluate. All of the major publishers and most of the midsized ones will only accept agented submissions. But finding an agent can be as difficult as finding a publisher. I receive 10 to 20 unsolicited query letters a day. (We call this "the slush pile"). From that, I might decide to represent only 5 to 10 projects in a given year. With all those query letters, you can probably expect the agent to spend about a minute on yours. So you will need to put some thought into composing that letter. And if the agent expresses an interest, you need to send the book proposal to him right away. He won't remember why he asked for the proposal if you respond in a month.

Authors seeking agent representation always seem to be fascinated and confused about how to write effective query letters. They are looking for some kind of formula, a magic bullet that will get the agent's attention. The most popular classes I give at writers conferences are workshops for composing query letters. I don't think it's an insuperable challenge, but most authors get it wrong.

Since agents are busy and the slush pile is big, the most frequent mistake I see with query letters is they are too long. You can't write a complete summary about what your book is and why it is important in a query letter. That will be the role of the book proposal. You have to describe the book and explain why it should be published in just a few sentences. Normally a query letter will have a three-part structure. The first paragraph will usually state the title, the genre, and the number of words in the manuscript (if you have completed it). Next you will have the main body of the query, where you explain what the book is and why it should be published. I prefer that it be written as briefly as possible. Some agents, though, want longer query letters. Agents will give you some indication of their preferences for length when you go to the submission page of the agent's website. The final paragraph should have something about yourself, what you do in the real world, and why you have the authority to write the book.

Always, always, always have a professional tone. When you say what genre your book is, make sure it is a term of art that is common in publishing. Don't say, for instance, your book is a "non-fiction novel." You'd be surprised how often I hear that. And this is not an impressive way to start a query letter.

Project an air of confidence, but don't overdo it. Sometimes I get queries that start off like this: "I really don't have much of a platform to write this book. I might have to self-publish it, but I thought I would show it to you first." Well, this certainly makes a convincing case for me not to want to represent it.

Authors usually ask me whether they should indicate that they are familiar with the agent and the agent's list. Some agents like this. I don't. Frequently I get queries that start by telling me how much they loved Cody's, my bookstore for many years. That's nice, but it always sounds a little like the author is just sucking up. Don't waste words with your query.

Avoid hype. Let me repeat that, because this is the most important point I will make in the book. Avoid hype. By now, you probably have intuited that I expect you to be honest. You might be seeking an agent who is a master of the wily arts of snake oil selling. If so, I'm not your man. Part of it is selfish. I need publishers to trust me. But also you need to be aware that agents and editors have pretty good bullshit detectors. We've seen every form of hype. And it sends a bad message. Either the writer has delusions of grandeur, or else he is dishonest. These aren't good qualities.

Here's a list of some common hypes:

- "There is nothing like this book that has ever been published." [This is one of the worst pitches you can make. It's a classic delusion of grandeur. And it also raises the reasonable question of whether there is a good reason why there is no other book like it.]

- "This book will sell millions of copies." [Really? NOT!]

- "This book will make a great movie." [I have never represented an author who didn't have unshakeable certainty that her book was headed for Hollywood. There are lots and lots of entertainment deals for "options." An option agreement is the right granted by the author to a producer that gives him an exclusive to sell the film rights to the book for a given period of time, usually a year, during which the producer will go hunting for a partner with the money and the power to produce the movie or TV show. Most of these options are sold for very little money. Most of them expire without a film deal. People in Hollywood don't think like you and me. The first question they will ask about a film adaptation of your book is: "How will this appeal to sixteen year olds?" The second question is usually something like "How much will the sets cost?"]

- "Oprah/Terry Gross will love this book." [My standard advice to clients is don't mention Oprah or Terry Gross.]

- "This book is like *Eat, Pray, Love* meets Malcolm Gladwell." [Publishers like this kind of appeal to dualisms. I don't know why. But I have seen far too many references to *Eat, Pray, Love* and Malcolm Gladwell in query letters in the slush pile. My response is to roll my eyes. *Eat, Pray, Love* has sold over 9,000,000 copies. Your book probably won't. This is another example of delusions of grandeur meets clumsy efforts at manipulation.]

- "This book was previously self-published and had very good sales." [Normally when I look into this further, I discover that the writer's idea of "very good sales" means about 500 copies, which is to say: "not very good sales". But even if your sales were good, if it turns out that you were selling an e-book for 99 cents or even giving it away for free, as is often the case, agents and editors won't be impressed.]

These kinds of pitches are dishonest and deceptive. I won't make this pitch to an editor, and you shouldn't make this pitch to me.

As an exercise in applying my rules for queries, I gave myself an almost insurmountable challenge, to create a query for one of the longest and most complex novels in the western canon and to try to describe the book and its importance in only a few sentences. Here is what I have described immodestly as "The Greatest Query Letter Ever Written."

I am submitting *War and Peace*, a 350,000 word work of historical fiction.

War and Peace is the epic story, written in a realistic style, of Napoleon's invasion of Russia and how 3 characters, members of the Russian nobility, live their lives or die in the course of the novel. In addition to the dramatic and interrelated stories of Pierre Bezukhov, Natasha Rostova, and Prince Andrei Bolkosky, I also bring in themes that try to explain how the events in the narrative help us to understand the inexorable truths of history. Some of the memorable secondary characters are real historical figures, notably Napoleon and the Russian general, Kutuzov. My description of the climactic Battle of Borodino is so realistic the reader can almost smell the gun powder.

The book has received enthusiastic praise from some of the most distinguished novelists of all time. Thomas Mann said of *War and Peace* that it was "the greatest war novel in the history of literature." John Galsworthy has called *War and Peace* "the best novel that had ever been written."

I am a published novelist, author of the best selling novel, *Anna Karenina* that has been translated into every major language in the world and adapted for film multiple times, most recently in 2012 from a screenplay by Tom Stoppard starring Keira Knightly and Jude Law. I have also written works of short stories, philosophy, and social criticism.

The manuscript is complete and available at your request.

Count Leo Tolstoy

Here's a real query letter I received from Jennifer Buhl, author of *Shooting Stars: My Unexpected Life Photographing Hollywood's Most Famous*. I called her up before I had even finished reading this one. How could I resist?

"I am seeking representation for my memoir: *Shooting Stars: My Unexpected Life Photographing Hollywood's Most Famous*, a tell-all book about today's hottest celebrities from the inside eyes of one of Hollywood's few female paparazzi.

Chock-full of celebrity anecdotes, *Shooting Stars*

WRITING A NON-FICTION BOOK PROPOSAL 11

provides an authoritative look into a world everyone's heard about, but few will ever experience. All of the tabloid favorites are here: Brit, Linds, Cam, Jen, Becks, Zac. Fans can read about how "paps" get the shot and the tricks some celebs use to keep us from getting it.

As a woman in a profession dominated by men and marked by ugliness, I struggled to gain acceptance while dealing with embarrassment, harassment, ridicule... and a rapidly ticking biological clock. Yes, woven among the true stories of my encounters with the world's most famous is my own story, the story of a woman in her mid-thirties looking for love, babies... and adrenaline.

The completed 115,000-word memoir spans my work as an L.A. paparazza from 2006 to 2009. Previous to that I worked as a CNN guest producer ("booker"). I have been a guest on CNN's Larry King Live and Nancy Grace, and on NPR, as well as other media outlets. My photographs have appeared copiously in publications and TV shows around the world, including TMZ, *People Magazine*, Britain's *Daily Mail*, and Entertainment Tonight. As a freelance photographer, I own the copyright to, and the right to reprint, all of my photos.

The first two chapters are pasted below and the full book will be available for review in early December. Thank you for your consideration."

I dug the following query letter by Mary Thompson-Jones out of the slush pile. I knew immediately I was interested in the book. It had such a strong premise. It was based on the WikiLeaks cables. But what impressed me the most was Mary's authority to write about the subject. She had been a high level diplomat and was now head of a prestigious academic program. She was also the author of over 300 of the cables. When I first read the query letter, I wasn't quite sure the book would work exactly as she described it. We had some long discussions about what aspects of the story would resonate best as a book. The final book is under a new name and is quite different from the original concept. It was published by W. W. Norton in July 2016.

This query is for a non-fiction, current affairs/ government book.

When the world awoke Nov. 28, 2010, to read the first of the WikiLeaks State Department cables, Italian Foreign Minister Franco Frattini warned, "It will be the September 11 of world diplomacy." *New York Times* Executive Editor Bill Keller said the five-week experience publishing the leaked cables felt as though "something—journalism, diplomacy, life as we know it— profoundly changed forever."

The WikiLeaks release astounded the world, but the diplomats who wrote the 251,287 cables remained largely mute. I know, because I was one of them. Some 300 of the WikiLeaks cables bear my signature, from the time I served as Chargé d'Affaires at the U.S. Embassy in Prague. As a 23-year veteran of the American diplomatic corps, I can reveal far more than journalists were able to uncover under deadline pressure. My proposed book: *WikiLeaks Diplomacy: Surprising Stories from the American Embassy Cables*, takes an in-depth look at the embassy reporting from 2006- 2010, the years covering most of the WikiLeaks cables.

Imagine reading how Kenya shipped planeloads full of wild animals to a Thai zoo in exchange for its vote to gain a U.N. Security Council seat; or what the streets of Port au Prince looked like seconds after the 2010 earthquake struck ("all I could see was dust and gasoline flowing down the road") or why Russian intellectuals insisted anti-Americanism is a "pillar" of its foreign policy. These cables, by turns outrageous, riveting, and insightful, are never boring. Given the proper foreign policy context, they add immeasurably to our knowledge of how the Bush and Obama administrations pursued foreign policy between 2006 and 2010.

I bring both insider diplomatic and academic credentials to this project. As a diplomat–and writer of some of the cables–I have the credibility to satisfy readers and the skills to interpret and connect them to American foreign policy. In the academic world, I am the director of the master's program in Global Studies and International Affairs at Northeastern University's College of Professional Studies, a position that affords me access to Boston's rich international affairs community. My dual role gives me a wide ranging author's platform.

I hope my topic intrigues you, and that you will consider representing me.

Authors always ask me whether they should include the book proposal with the query letter and whether it should be an attachment or embedded in the body of the letter. They also want to know whether the query should be sent by mail or electronically. I always advise referring to the submission page of an agent's website. Each agent will have his own preferences.

Finding an Agent

> A writer died and was given the option of going to heaven or hell. She decided to check out each place first.
>
> As the writer descended into the fiery pits, she saw row upon row of writers chained to their desks in a steaming sweatshop. As they worked, they were repeatedly whipped with thorny lashes.
>
> "Oh my," said the writer. "Let me see heaven now."
>
> A few moments later, as she ascended into heaven, she saw rows of writers, chained to their desks in a steaming sweatshop. As they worked, they, too, were whipped with thorny lashes.
>
> "Wait a minute," said the writer. "This is just as bad as hell!"
>
> "Oh no, it's not," replied her guide.
>
> "Come on!" she protested. "What's the difference?"
>
> "Here," the guide said, "the writers have agents."

Reputable literary agents work on commission only, usually 15% of all revenue flowing to the author from the book and all derivatives of the book (licenses, abridgements, TV/film rights, mugs and T-shirts, to name just a few). You should avoid agents who require you to pay them an up-front fee. It's probably a scam.

If you have to give the agent that big a commission, you ought to at least make him work for it. A good agent will evaluate your idea and try to refine it. A good agent will edit your book proposal to make sure it addresses the concerns of the publisher and presents the most convincing case for your project. A good agent can tell you whether your concept needs to be changed. The biggest problem I see with proposals that are otherwise worthy is when the author seems to be smitten with two ideas and is trying to shoe horn both of them into a single project. I work with the author to define what the best idea is and to convince him to save the others for his next book, (or, more often than not, just discard it forever).

A great proposal is one that anticipates the questions the editor will be asking and provides compelling but honest answers to those questions. Every agent has gotten thousands of rejection letters from acquisition editors for projects he represents. Rejection is painful for us as well as for you. But those rejections teach us what publishers are looking for, what questions they are asking, and what answers inspire them to make an offer.

Let me briefly outline the procedure for researching agents. It's easy to be intimidated by this, but it really is quite simple. Before you begin, I recommend checking out the website and blog: "Writer Beware" (sfwa.org/other-resources/for-authors/writer-beware /). It's run by the Science Fiction and Fantasy Writers Association. It gives excellent advice on how to avoid bad agents.

After you have composed a stunning query letter, it's time to assemble a list of agents. There are a number of good data bases to help you. You can easily find them online. The most exclusive list is the membership of the Association of Author Representatives or AAR (aaronline.org/Find), the trade association of dramatic and literary agents. In order to become a member of AAR, you must have sold a considerable number of books in an 18-month period and must agree to a code of ethics. A larger list is on agentquery.com. I recommend this site to prospective authors. You can select agents based on the specific interests and genres the agents are seeking. It will also provide useful thumbnail information about the agent and list the genres he represents. All of the listings have links to the agents' websites. Some agents will say they are not seeking new clients. Don't waste your time with them.

After you assemble your initial list, go to each website for further research. The websites usually have more biographical information about the agents, subjective material about what kinds of projects turn them on, lists of books and authors they represent, and submission guidelines. Remember agents are inveterate name droppers. They will trumpet their big name clients and brag about all their six and seven figure deals. Don't get intimidated by this. Agents are always looking for new talent as well.

I have had the same anxieties when meeting new book editors. When first I visited Rachel Klayman, executive editor at Crown Books, I asked her what kinds of books she was acquiring. She responded that probably her best known author was Barack Obama. I was pretty cowed. But she still calls me up and asks me if I have anything cool to submit.

Once you have a list of 20-30 potential agents, send out your query letters. Send them simultaneously. Some agents will respond in a few days, some in weeks, some never. Don't wait for all their responses. After a month or two, send out your next list. You will probably get many rejections, but don't despair. That's show business. Or as Nat King Cole famously said: "Pick yourself up. Dust yourself off. Start all over again."

If you aren't a celebrity and your project doesn't have an obvious mass market, you might want to stay clear of some of these big name agents. I have a number of clients who had previous representation from high profile agents, and they were not well served. Don't get me wrong. Some of them are quite good. But others are too busy, too lazy, or too greedy to work hard on a project that might net them a very small commission. If you are a debut author, it is going to be tough to get a big advance or even a contract with one of the big five publishers. If your goal is to find the right home for your book, even if that home is a smaller publisher and the advance is modest, you need to engage an agent who is willing to do that. You would be better served by a newer agent, one who is building his list and is willing to take some chances. I once represented an author who had written a book I loved, but I couldn't find a publisher for it. I sent it to about forty houses. No luck. Finally, after three years, I found a publisher. The author got a $1,000 advance. I received a $150 commission. But I don't think I have ever been happier or more fulfilled than when I sold that book. That's the kind of work you want your agent to do.

The other way to find agents is to attend writers conferences and "agent pitch" sessions organized by writers groups. The best place to look for a comprehensive list of these conferences is on the Poets and Writers website (www.pw.org/conferences_and_residencies). The conferences are usually fun, sometimes in cool locations, and there are always agents around to pitch to. If you meet an agent at a conference and he asks you to send him material, the agent will usually put it at the top of his pile and give you a little extra consideration. If you don't have a specific project to pitch or if yours isn't ready for submission, that's ok. Use your pitch time to get valuable advice from the agent about how book publishing works, what kind of input they can give on the concept of your project, or even some tips on writing book proposals or query letters.

Living With Rejection

> "The struggle itself towards the heights is enough to fill a man's heart."
> —Albert Camus, *The Myth of Sisyphus*

Rejection is a big part of this business and you need to live with it. After you get rejected by 30 agents and you find one who loves your book, your rejections have still just begun. Typically for any proposal I am representing, I will do the research and submit to as many as 40 publishers. I might get 2 offers, 1 offer, or no offers. I hate it too. Sometimes it feels like my social life in high school.

Agents act as filters for the book industry. We make sure the projects that get to an editor's desk are solid and good enough to be published. But publishers make acquisition decisions that often have little to do with the quality of your project. Sometimes they have another book like yours on their list, and they don't want to compete with their own title. Sometimes they have had bad experiences with a similar book, and they don't want to risk another. Sometimes they are scared off by modest sales of your previous book. Sometimes it just doesn't turn the editor on.

I did a blog about rejection once that had an enormous number of views. It was called "Publisher Rejection Letters From Plato to Hitler" (andy-rossagency.wordpress.com / 2010 / 02 / 13 /publisher-rejection-letters-from-plato-to-hitler/). In the blog I took phrases from real rejection letters as I imagined they would be used to turn down books like: *War and Peace*, *Macbeth*, *Ulysses*, and *Mein Kampf*. (*Mein Kampf* came about the closest to getting published. They liked Hitler's platform.)

You've heard all the stories about the great books that have been rejected. *Harry Potter, Catch 22, The Diary of Anne Frank, Gone With the Wind, Animal Farm, Dune*. It's a long list. I once asked an editor what was the biggest mistake she ever made. She rejected *Men are from Mars, Women are from Venus*. The book went on to sell over 10 million copies worldwide. Bummer!

I guess what I want to tell you, and there's no way to sugar coat this, is that there is a lot of rejection in this business, and you need to go into it with clear eyes. There's always a good chance I won't be able to find a publisher for your book. My advice is to shake it out, and move on to the next project. Remember that writing is not just a job; it's a vocation, a calling. The activity itself opens your heart to the world and rewards you in ways that are rich, and ineffable. Publication is a business transaction. And it probably won't make you rich or famous. Think about that final unforgettable line from *The Myth of Sisyphus* by Albert Camus: "The struggle itself towards the heights is enough to fill a man's heart." As writers, this has to be our motto.

What is Platform?

The first thing an agent or an editor will be looking for is the author's "platform." The obsession with platform has become ubiquitous in book publishing. And in the course of writing your book proposal, you are going to have to face up to it. We are living in a world driven by media. And the reality is in this environment, who you are is often just as important as what you are writing.

Platform is your reputation in the real world. It includes your authority to write about the subject of your book and your ability to get the media attention it takes to promote it. I like to tell people platform is one of two things. It's either an endowed chair at Harvard or you are sleeping with Oprah's hair dresser. (Both would be preferable.)

There is a lot of nonsense about "platform" floating around. You hear it from motivational speakers at writers conferences, and you read it in "tip" pieces in magazines and blogs directed at writers. There are platform gurus who consult with you and charge hefty fees to tell you how to "create your own platform."

There is really nothing wrong with this advice. Most of these tips are true to an extent and useful. Yes, you might find it helpful to set up a blog; and when your book gets published God willing, you will need to have a website. You should mine the social media. Facebook is *de rigueur*. Some people swear by Twitter; although when I set up my Twitter account, I only seemed to get invitations from prostitutes.

The problem is most of this advice is motivational, inspired by the gospel of "positive thinking," and often promises more than it can deliver. The subtext is if you follow a few simple tips, you can develop a platform that will be the key to getting your book published and promoted. This is not necessarily true. Book publishers have set a very high bar for platform. A robust platform is not just a blog, a website, and a Twitter account.

Take blogs, for instance. Publishers have higher expectations than the rest of us for what constitutes a successful blog. I have a blog. You should all read it. It's called "Ask the Agent" (andyrossagency.word press.com). It's popular. It works pretty well as a blog. I get about 8000 views a month. That's over 500,000 views in the life of the blog. But it wouldn't impress a publisher, at least not enough to influence their decision to produce a book. If you have 50,000 views a month, it would get their attention. But still, it isn't going to be the final determinant in the acquisition decision. And don't forget. You can't just recycle your blog material into a book. If it's already available for free online, why would anyone want to pay $25 to read the same material in book form?

A syndicated *New York Times* columnist has an impressive platform. A columnist for *The Des Moines Register*—maybe not so much—unless the book is about hog confinements. A holder of a chaired professorship at a prestigious university has an impressive platform.

(Publishers seem to love Harvard. I don't know why.) But still this platform is only significant if she is writing in her specialized field and only if the subject is going to interest a wide non-academic audience. A Nobel laureate has an impressive platform and can pretty much pontificate about any old nonsense that suits his fancy. A Pulitzer Prize winner has an impressive plat-form, but he also needs a book idea a publisher thinks will make money. I've gotten rejections from publish-ers for books by Pulitzer Prize winners. Lots of them.

A television or media personality has an impressive platform. But if his audience is regional, that reduces the value of his platform. Publishers are wary of re-gional titles. Almost all book editors live and work in New York. And they tend to see books about New York City as "national." Everything else is "regional." That might explain why there are so many cookbooks associated with trendy restaurants in Brooklyn. Nation-al media celebrities, especially those with a certain kind of reputation, especially those whose tawdry personal lives you read about while standing in line at Safeway, especially those who have no reason for being famous other than the fact that they are famous—now that is the platinum standard for platform. If I were the agent for the Sisters Kardashian, I'd be on easy street. I could af-ford a Rolex watch. I might even be able to buy a diamond pinky ring.

As an agent, the first thing I want to know when I read a query letter is "what is the author's platform." Does she have the authority to write about the subject of her book? More importantly, will that authority be recognized by a national readership. An acquisition editor will be asking the same question.

Sometimes you just can't make a silk purse out of a sow's ear. If you don't have a platform, don't pretend you do. A good book proposal is an honest book proposal. And that leads us to:

The Mind of the Acquisition Editor

An editor's life isn't all that glamorous. She (and it's usually a she) works in a 10' x 10' office all day, every day. She has to attend boring acquisition meetings with a bunch of other editors who are pitching their pet projects for the same slot in the catalogue as hers. The publisher, the sales director, and the marketing manager are all there too. Maybe they have read your proposal. Maybe they have only read the first page. Maybe they have only read your agent's pitch letter. Maybe the marketing director had a fight with his wife the night before, or he just found out his kid didn't get into Harvard. And that person could very well veto your project. It's just a fact of life.

Every acquisition editor gets 10-20 proposals a week. Every one of those proposals has been selected by an agent only after a robust vetting process. Almost all of them will have a compelling reason to get published. But the editor will probably only be allowed to publish 10 to 20 books a year. So you have some pretty stiff competition.

The dirty little secret of book acquisition is that it's pretty subjective. I mean it probably is a little more businesslike than your kid's lemonade stand. When I talk to an editor, they almost always use the expression "falling in love" (not with me, but with the book). Recently I did an interview with book editor Peter Ginna where we discussed the role of the editor in the book publication process. Peter is editor and contributor to What Editors Do: The Art, Craft, and Business of Book Editing, published by The University of Chicago Press. The book is an anthology of essays by 27 of the most respected editors in publishing talking about their work from acquisition to publication. Any writer considering publishing with a major press should read this book. Peter has been a book editor for over 30 years. He has worked at Bloomsbury USA, Oxford University Press, Crown Publishers, and St. Martin's Press. Authors he has worked with include James McPherson, David Hackett Fischer, David Oshinsky, Daniel Ellsberg (my client), and Suze Orman. Check out Peter's blog on writing and publishing: "Doctor Syntax."

Andy: Peter, what I hear from almost every writer who has not yet been published is "editors don't edit any more". I'm sure you've heard it too. Is this true? If not, can you speculate on why this attitude is so prevalent?

Peter: Sigh... I've been hearing this complaint since I got into publishing in the 1980s. All I can say is that every editor I know spends many, many hours of their nights and weekends editing—it's almost impossible to find time do it in the office. As I say in my book, working on manuscripts is still the core and defining function for most of us. I have edited almost every title I've published, usually line by line. And if I haven't, somebody else has. That said, there have always been some editors who didn't edit much, or even edited badly. And the economic pressures today to get more titles out of fewer editors sometimes means some books don't get as much attention as they deserve. But it's pretty frustrating for those of us who wear our #2 pencils down to little stubs on people's manuscripts when we hear this comment tossed off so casually.

Andy: I have to tell you that my life as an agent can be frustrating. I get so many rejections from editors. Lately, I've been doing a lot of literary fiction and some literary memoir. Tough genres, I know. But everything I take on is special in one way or another. And I still get a massive amount of rejections. At the same time, I see things getting published that just aren't that good. In literary fiction, I see books that are well written and well crafted, but they seem kind of the same. What should I tell my heartbroken and talented client after he gets his 30th rejection?

Peter: "Thirty-first time's the charm!" Seriously, publishing has always been a subjective, hit-or-miss business. No book is to everybody's taste, or every editor's, and sometimes unexceptional work finds its way into print. And anyone who knows publishing history knows that some wonderful and even bestselling books were rejected many times before publication. I would tell authors what I bet you already say: "It only takes one." One editor who loves what you're doing and can communicate his passion to the publishing house.

Andy: Whenever I give presentations before authors' groups, I try to be brutally honest about the realistic chances of getting published. Let's talk about your batting averages. When you were an editor at Bloomsbury, how many book proposals did you typically get a week? How many were agented (heavily vetted)? How many were good enough to get published? How many did you publish in a year?

Peter: Whew, that's a lot of questions. I would guess I got between 15-30 submissions a week; probably 80 percent of those were agented, because I wasn't fielding total slush submissions (meaning those addressed to "Dear Bloomsbury"). I acquired 15 to 20 new titles a year, out of all of those.

Andy: Hmm. Let's see. That's about 1,000 proposals a year and you published maybe 15. I'll try not to take it so personally next time I get a rejection from an editor. And of those titles you published, how many ended up making money?

Peter: Probably around a third or fewer turned a profit for the house in the first few years, though my list was generally oriented toward books that, with luck, would backlist and generate money over the long term.

Andy: Most of the people reading this interview are thinking about how to go about finding an agent. Can you give them some advice? What should they be looking for?

Peter: My feeling is there are two key things a writer should look for in an agent. First, do they truly get my work—do they understand what I'm trying to do and know how to help me realize it? (Some agents, and some editors I'm afraid, try to squeeze a writer or a book into a form or category that they think will be saleable, but that is at odds with what the author is really trying to accomplish.) Second and equally important, do I have the right relationship, the right chemistry, with this agent? Not only do I trust them, which is critical, but is their style of doing business going to mesh with mine? Agents come in all shapes and sizes and personalities—some are very warm and fuzzy, some are cool and clinical. Either one can be highly effective but if you are not comfortable with it, it's a bad match.

Andy: The one thing I hear that makes me see red is a writer who only wants to have a New York agent. Do they really have an edge? Is there some kind of alchemical magic that happens at the Publisher's Lunch?

Peter: I don't think the agent's location is important. If you were in New York, I'd enjoy having lunch with you more often, but as an editor it is much more important to me that you (a) always had high-quality submissions and never wasted my time and (b) were always professional and a straight shooter. Those are the qualities that get an agent's clients favorable attention from a publisher, not whether the agent is in Manhattan.

Andy: In your book, Jon Karp says the first rule for an editor is "Love it." This seems a little squishy soft for all you tough minded guys working for multi-media conglomerates. Is Jon maybe romanticizing his job a little bit?

Peter: Absolutely not, and I was struck by how many of the contributors to *What Editors Do* make that same point (including me). Publishing any book requires an enormous investment of time and psychic energy by an editor. The process takes months and sometimes years. If you make that kind of commitment to a book you're not really passionate about, it becomes a total grind and you often end up hating yourself for it. You don't have to "love" every book the same way—a book on how to restore furniture isn't the same as a lyrical literary novel. But you have to feel something in your heart or your gut that says this book is a special one of its kind. My own name for that feeling is "**the spark**." As an editor it's your job to pass that spark on to others in house, and then out to readers in the outside world.

Andy: But still, as the cliché goes, book publishing is the marriage of art and commerce. So once you "love it," you have to take it through the meat grinder. Can you tell us the next steps you go through before the publisher makes the acquisition decision?

Peter: Here's where I plug my product and note that I go through the whole process in detail in my chapter on acquisitions. The procedures vary considerably from house to house—at a small indie publisher, unsurprisingly, it's less bureaucratic than at a Big Five corporation. But essentially, you share the material with your colleagues and try to get support for the project, especially from departments like publicity, marketing, sales, and sub rights who will be tasked with selling the thing if you sign it up. And you have to figure out how much money the house should invest in the project, which involves doing a projected profit and loss statement—the infamous P&L.

Andy: Ok. So let's talk about the P&L. It's always been a puzzlement to me. Can you describe this? How on earth can you make realistic sales projections on a product that is unique? Sure, you can do it for a test guide, or Lee Child's next Reacher novel. But what about a book like, say, Daniel Ellsberg's *The Doomsday Machine*, which was acquired for Bloomsbury by you, Peter)?

Peter: Aha, this is the $64,000 question! In some sense what publishers do is reinvent the wheel a hundred times a year, because just as you say, every product is unique. That makes it really hard to project sales figures with any sense of certainty. The best you can do is make educated guesses about what a new title is likely to sell, based on the author's track record, sales of comparable titles, likely media interest, and possibly the casting of horoscopes or Tarot cards. Plus, of course, people's response to the manuscript or proposal itself. Once you have made a sales projection, the P&L is—in theory—simply a straightforward calculation of the revenue generated by those sales, less the costs of royalties, printing, distribution and so on. Each house will have some target for what percentage of profit must be left at the end of the day.

Andy: It's always mystified me how you come up with the final number for an advance. The only thing consistent is that it is usually too low. Can you describe what goes into the calculation?

Peter: Well, what the editor **wants** to offer as an advance is the author's royalty earnings as generated on the P&L just mentioned—or preferably a lower number that allows the author to earn out even if sales fall short of the projection—as they often do. But note that in referring to the P&L numbers I said **"in theory."** Your P&L needs to show X percent profit, whatever advance you are offering. But suppose you are in a competitive situation, bidding against other publishers for a hot book. Very often, you wind up re-projecting your sales figures so that you can still show a profit on the P&L when the advance goes from $50,000 to $250,000 or whatever.

Andy: So cutting to the chase, is there a quick and dirty rule of thumb to estimate how big an advance you would offer for a specific estimated hardback sale? One editor said that an estimate of 10,000 copies sold will translate into a $25,000 advance. Does this seem reasonable?

Peter: I don't know about "rule of thumb." It's more like basic arithmetic. I always just figured it out by multiplying the likely royalty per copy by whatever number we were expecting/hoping to sell. If you figure a 10% royalty on a $25 book, that's $2.50 a copy, so that gets you your $25K if you sell 10,000 copies. Obviously, that's not totally accurate because the royalty would go to 12.5% at 5000 copies, which would earn more than $25K. But of course in reality you might sell less than 10,000 or the list price might be less than $25, so it makes a viable ballpark number. Figuring a 10 percent royalty just makes the math simpler to do.

Andy: And then there is the word that is on everyone's lips in book publishing: "Platform." What is easier to get published: a pretty good book by a guy with great platform or a really good book by a guy without it?

Peter: I'm afraid it will almost always be easier to get the pretty good book published by the guy with a great platform. (However, the really good book may well outsell it in the end.) People love to hate the word "platform," but it's just shorthand for an author's ability to command attention in the marketplace, which publishers have always been keenly aware of, and rightly so. This could mean either the attention of readers who already know the author, or the attention of intermediaries (media, celebrities, scholars, peers in their field, *etc.*) who will in turn alert those readers. So "platform" could be access to Oprah or a ton of Twitter or Instagram followers, or a syndicated column.

Andy: So what's your advice to my platform challenged authors?

Peter: I'd say rather than getting hung up on this idea of platform, think of it this way: How do you mobilize the community of interest around you and your subject? What's going to get people who care about this to spread the word about the book? You should start this mobilizing from the moment you begin work on the book—don't wait until your book is in galleys to start building relationships and raising your profile. I remember reading a proposal for a biography of Jesse James by a first-time author. He had no major public credentials, but he had managed to get a very strong endorsement of his work from James M. McPherson, a Pulitzer-winning and bestselling historian. I instantly took his proposal seriously. Alas for me, it was bought by Knopf. That author, T.J. Stiles, has now won the Pulitzer Prize himself, twice!

Andy: In this book, probably my most important message that a great book proposal is one that anticipates the questions the acquisition editor will be asking. Am I right? How important are book proposals in your acquisition decision?

Peter: Especially in nonfiction, book proposals are critical. No matter how good your platform is, you need a strong proposal that makes clear why your subject will be compelling to readers and what you have to say about it that's not available elsewhere. You are exactly right that the author should answer the questions the editor is going to ask. And the first question is generally, if crudely, expressed as, "So what?" What am I, the reader, going to come away with if I invest twenty-five or so dollars, and more important, several hours of my time, in reading this book? If you've answered that, you're well on the way to having a good proposal.

What Happens When I Get an Offer?

Okay. The editor has fallen in love with your proposal. He has shown it around the office and taken it to the acquisition meeting. His boss has given it the thumbs up. My phone rings. It's the editor telling me everybody loves the project. He wants to make an offer. Next he will likely start sounding defensive and kind of squirmy, hemming and hawing, and then explains to me why the advance he is offering is insultingly low. Afterwards, he will send me a formal offer that includes a number of deal points.

When a publisher makes an offer for your book, it's usually not just for the work in book form. It is a license to publish the book and exploit the material in the book for the term of the copyright (life of the author plus 70 years). The deal points include advance, hardback royalties, paperback royalties, e-book royalties, territory (what countries and what languages they can sell the book in), and lots of subsidiary rights like abridgments, audio, excerpts, and book clubs. It might also include an offer for rights for merchandise like T-shirts, calendars, and coffee mugs. Usually the author can reserve film/TV/performance rights and sell them separately.

A Word About the "Advance"

Authors and publishers love to talk about advances. Authors want big ones, and publishers want them as small as possible and the payments spread over time. Originally the purpose of the advance was to give authors money to live on while they were writing the book. This is rarely the case anymore. Most advances are less than $20,000, and they are almost never paid as a lump sum on signing the contract. Typically advances will be paid in multiple parts based on specified mile posts in the publishing process. Smaller advances (usually under $30,000) are paid in two equal parts; 50% on signing and the rest on delivery and acceptance of the complete manuscript. Larger advances will have a third pay-out on publication. The largest ones will often have an additional portion paid on publication of the paperback. This isn't even an advance. More of a "behind" (pun intended).

Still, the advance is the metric all people in publishing use as a shorthand to describe the importance of a particular book deal. A good advance, over $100,000, is usually referred to as a six figure deal. A great advance, as a seven figure deal. Sadly, I have had a number of advances that have been in the "low four figures." Not big enough to brag about at a fancy literary cocktail party.

The Elements of the Book Deal

Let's go over the deal points one by one. We've already talked about the advance and the payout of the advance. Here are some other elements that play a part in the book deal.

- **Hardback royalties**. Authors have to earn their income from book sales the good old fashion way. They receive a royalty on every book sold. The advance is exactly that, an advance against royalties. Any advance money you receive prior to publication is going to be deducted from the royalties you amass as the book sells. You won't receive any royalty payments until your total royalties (or other income) exceeds the amount of the advance. Publishers call this "earning out." Most books never earn out.

  The typical hardback royalty for a book from a major publisher is 10% of list (cover) price for the first 5000 sold, 12.5% for next 5000, and 15% thereafter. Many books get discounted now, particularly if they are being sold online. But that won't affect your royalty. Smaller publishers often have smaller royalty rates.

- **Paperback royalties**. Often publishers will put out a paperback edition of a book after a year. The theory is that by then, the hardback sales will have run their course, and there might be a new audience for a cheaper edition. Royalties on paperbacks are always lower. Most publishers have a flat rate of 7.5% of list price. Sometimes I can get them to give a larger royalty rate if the book sells more than 10-20,000 copies.

- **E-book royalties**. E-books became a major factor in publisher in 2007 when Amazon.com released its first Kindle Reader. For the next five years, it seemed like all anyone wanted to talk about was e-books. Sales of e-books grew exponentially as sales for traditional format books declined. Many of us in book publishing started to believe that the Age of Gutenberg was coming to an end, and books printed on paper were going to go the way of the clay tablet. Then in 2012, the growth rate for e-books published by commercial publishers flattened out, and in 2015 they declined for the first time. Now e-books constitute about 20% of the unit sales of most major publishers.

  Typically, publishers give a royalty of 25% of net on e-book sales. The term "net" means the amount of money that is actually received by publishers. Most authors and agents believe that this rate is unfair to authors. It's usually less than the author would receive for a hardback book. And e-books are substantially cheaper to produce and distribute. There are no costs for printing, warehousing, and shipping, and there are almost no returns.

- **Territory**. Part of the book deal includes what territories the publisher will be allowed to sell into or license the sale of the book. Publishers usually want "world rights." The right to sell the book throughout the world. Authors and agents frequently prefer to sell rights only for North American English and work out deals with other publishers in other countries and in other languages.

- **Subsidiary Rights**. The book deal is much more than the sale of a book to the publisher. It is a license to exploit the material in the book in any way that is specified in the contract. There are usually long lists of subsidiary rights which include: abridgements, serialization, excerpts, anthologies, verbatim and non-verbatim apps and multimedia rights, audio rights, and merchandise rights. Usually the publisher and author split the income from these rights 50/50.

- And then, of course, there is the ever popular **Movie/TV/Performance Rights**. Most publishers allow authors to reserve those rights.

The author can negotiate entertainment deals separately. Movie contracts are byzantine in their complexity and we won't go into the details now. Suffice it to say that many hours are spent wrangling over the number of tickets the agent will receive to the premier and the payment for the right to erect a ride in a theme park derived from the book. (Now if you'll excuse me, Steven Spielberg is on my other line. I have a movie deal to make.)

The Book Contract

Once the deal points are decided upon, the publisher will send you the book contract to sign. A good agent will be able to recognize the roadside bombs in a book contract and negotiate some of them away. In a sentence, a book contract is an asymmetrical agreement written by the publisher that allows them to exploit your book in all defined ways for the term of the copyright; and in exchange, they will give you some chump change.

The Structure of the Book Proposal

Now let's get down to the nitty gritty. How do you write a book proposal? Most agents and publishers want proposals written on a Word document, but some agents prefer the proposal embedded in the email below the text of the query letter. (Most agents require electronic submissions.) The document should be double-spaced in 12 point Times New Roman font. It should include a title page. Following this, you should provide a "proposal table of contents" that has the page number for each of the sections of the proposal. Remember when you are doing your research for a list of agents, you must check out their websites. All agent websites have a "submission" page specifying details about how they want you to send query letters and book proposals. Here is the submission page on my website   (www.andyrossagency.com/submissions. html).

One of the first questions authors ask me is whether they should write the proposal in first or third person. You can do either. I prefer first person. It's more personal, more honest, more direct, and has a more natural voice. I dislike politicians, for example, who refer to themselves in the third person. It just sounds pretentious. And by all means, unless you are multiple authors (or the Queen of England), avoid the imperial "we."

The Title

Titles are important and it's worth putting some time into creating a good one. Non-fiction titles are usually in a standard format. There is the main title which should have a catchy or poetic quality and a subtitle which is more descriptive of the text. One of my favorite titles of a client's book is *Beasts: What Animals Can Teach Us About the Origins of Good and Evil* by Jeffrey Moussaieff Masson, published by Bloomsbury Press, 2014. We had trouble coming up with the title. We thought about it for over a year, before the publisher settled on this one. The sub-title is clear and doesn't require much explanation. But the title has an ironic double meaning. On the one hand, it tells us the book is about animals. But we also know the word "beast" is frequently used in a pejorative sense. This book attempts to show that humans, in our treatment of animals and of each other, are the real beasts.

Every book contract gives the publisher the final right to determine the title of the book. The author is often given the opportunity to consult. This probably makes sense. Titles are, above all else, a marketing tool. There is a story of a humorist in the 1950s who learned that three subjects were always popular: books about sex, books about cats, and books about the Third Reich. So he wrote a book called *Sex for Cats* and put a swastika on the cover. Now that's savvy marketing!

The Overview

The Overview introduces your project to the acquisition editor. You need to define in a few sentences a clear concept of the book and then go on to explain in your own words what the book is, why it is important and relevant, and why you are the right person to be the author of this book. It's also the place where you want to get the editor or the agent excited. Just like in a good novel, the reader is going to make about 75% of his decision by the end of the first page. So it's important to hook the editor right out of the gate.

Most writers I work with ask me how long The Overview needs to be. My response is it needs to be as long as it needs to be in order to answer the questions the editor will be asking. But since all editors and agents are busy, it shouldn't be longer than 10 pages double spaced. Shorter is better. Two pages? Mmmmm. Maybe that's too short.

When possible, I like to begin The Overview with an anecdote from the book, sometimes even a quote or a particularly dramatic paragraph that gives the editor/agent an emotional attachment to your project. It's called "the hook." If you are writing any kind of narrative non-fiction where you are trying to tell a story, your writing style is going to be almost as important as the content of the narrative. So you need to be able to show you have the ability to convey the drama in your writing. I tell people that the "how" is as important as the "what."

Below is a good example of a first paragraph. It's from *Water 4.0: The Past, Present, and Future of the World's Most Vital Resource* by David Sedlak, published by Yale University Press in 2014. The book is considered the definitive book on how we provide drinking water to cities and what the future holds. The "hook" in this proposal was particularly challenging. The author is a hydrological engineer, and there is a considerable amount of engineering and chemistry within the book. But Yale decided the book would be targeted to a general audience. David and I tried to find the most dramatic anecdote in the text that pointed out the crisis in the delivery of drinking water.

"In 2008, the city of Brisbane, Australia came within ten months of running out of water. Think about it: a city of over 2 million people in a developed country found itself unable to provide its citizens with water. After exhausting all of the normal remedies— shorter showers, brown lawns and dirty cars—the city invested over $700 million in a network of treatment plants capable of converting seawater and sewage into drinking water. But even with these new water sources, the future of Brisbane's drinking water supply remains in jeopardy as population growth, climate change and the discovery of new drinking water contaminants put additional pressure on the city's drinking water supply."

Here's another example from *Showstoppers!: The Surprising Backstage Stories of Broadway's Most Remarkable Songs* by Gerald Nachman published by Chicago Review Press in 2016. This first paragraph doesn't rely on a specific anecdote or event. But it's a powerful opening nonetheless. After all, your first paragraph is going to have to be a "showstopper" in its own right.

"When Robert Preston shouted "Ya got trouble!" in River City, when Carol Channing glided down a gilded staircase while waiters serenaded her with *Hello, Dolly!*, when Barbra Streisand defied us to rain on her parade in *Funny Girl*, when Joel Grey bid us "willkommen" and beckoned us into his seedy club, audiences were instantly enchanted. After such indelible moments, musicals were never the same; and neither were we."

One last example. This is one of my favorites. It's the opening to the proposal of *Surviving Paradise: One Year on a Disappearing Island* by Peter Rudiak-Gould published by Union Square Press in 2009.

"A month after my twenty-first birthday, I became romantically entangled with an island. Ujae was a third-of-a-square-mile-large, ocean-flat speck of land 70 miles from the nearest telephone, car, store, or tourist, and 2000 miles from the nearest continent–a backwater in the already obscure Marshall Islands. The island's 450 inhabitants still fished with spears, practiced jungle medicine, and sailed in breadfruit-wood canoes. I wanted Ujae to be my far-off utopia. Ujae wanted me to be its English teacher. So we married and we met, in that order."

Although this first paragraph is not particularly dramatic–publishers would probably call it "quiet"–the style is magnificent, the language is powerful and evocative and conveys the exotic quality of this place-based memoir telling the story of Peter's year in one of the most remote locations on earth.

Ok. So now you have the editor hooked. Maybe it's time to tell him exactly what your book is about. This isn't as easy as it sounds. You need to start the second paragraph (sometimes the first, if you can't find a good hook) by providing an "elevator pitch." This is a truly loathsome term of art. It originated in Hollywood. Presumably when you meet a big time producer in the elevator, you need to be able to tell him what your project is before arriving on the second floor. Some people say you have to define your project in a single sentence. I'll cut you a little slack and let you do it in two or three. But you still have to do it, glib though it may sound. And when I see elevator pitches that are too complicated, too abstract, or too vague, it usually means to me the writer either (1) doesn't have a clear idea of his own subject or (2) is trying to squeeze several different book ideas into a single project. One of my jobs as an agent is to identify this kind of problem and work with the author to clarify what the book is going to be about and which subject is the best idea to proceed with.

You hear the phrase "high concept" a lot in publishing these days. What it means is that concept of the book is so clear that you can comprehend it, usually with a single sentence description. My client, Doctor Steven Hatch's book: *Inferno: A Doctor's Ebola Story* is his memoir of treating Ebola patients in Liberia during the height of the great epidemic. That's a high concept. The one sentence description tells you clearly what the book is about. Another book I represent, Jennifer Buhl's *Shooting Stars: My Unexpected Life Photographing Hollywood's Most Famous*, is a memoir of the author's five years as a successful paparazzi. That's also a high concept book.

All books don't have "high concepts," and books that do aren't necessarily better. One of my favorite memoirs is *Wild* by Cheryl Strayed. You could describe it as the story of Cheryl's hiking the Pacific Crest Trail and, in the process, struggling to understand and overcome her own life failures. My description, although accurate, doesn't tell us the complexity and beauty of this remarkable book. *Wild* doesn't have a high concept. And that's one of its many virtues.

You may find it simplistic or even offensive to reduce your complex story into just a few sentences. But remember, one of the functions of the proposal is to give the editor ammunition to sell it to the rest of the decision-makers of the imprint at the acquisition meeting. And then the editorial department will have to excite the sales department. Then the sales reps will be travelling around the country trying to sell it to the bookseller. And the bookseller will have to sell it to the consumer. I was a bookseller for 35 years. I did most of the buying for my store, Cody's Books in Berkeley. The sales rep usually had about a minute to pitch the book to me. A good elevator pitch would serve him in good stead.

Below are some examples of elevator pitches in proposals written by my clients. As you will see, I've given them some flexibility to deviate from the classic one-line elevator pitch. Here's the first paragraph from *Chain of Title: How Three Ordinary Americans Uncovered Wall Street's Great Foreclosure Fraud* by David Dayen published in 2016 by The New Press.

"This is a story about three Floridians—Lisa Epstein, Michael Redman and Lynn Szymoniak—who helped to uncover the largest consumer fraud in American history. They didn't work in government or law enforcement. They were not experts in the judiciary. They had no history of anti-corporate activism or community organizing. Instead, they were all in foreclosure, and while struggling with the shame and dislocation and financial stress that causes, they committed a revolutionary act: they read their mortgage documents, and discovered one of Wall Street's darkest secrets."

David decided to opt out of starting with a "hook" and went right into the elevator pitch. The concept of the story is dramatic enough. If you were an elevator pitch purist, you might have written: "This story is *Erin Brockovich* meets *A Civil Action*." Or: "This is a David and Goliath story about the largest consumer fraud in American history, the Florida foreclosure scandal." I used both of those shortened phrases when I was pitching the book to publishers. "David and Goliath story" is a Hollywood term of art for a particular genre of movie where a scrappy everyman triumphs over an overpowering evil. Think *Erin Brockovich, Mr. Smith Goes To Washington*, and the greatest one of all–*Star Wars*. It's always nice to be able to frame a pitch that brings to mind an iconic film.

Here's another elevator pitch for *Shooting Stars: My Unexpected Life Photographing Hollywood's Most Famous* by Jennifer Buhl published by Sourcebooks in 2014.

"Thus begins my three-year career as a paparazza. *Shooting Stars: My Unexpected Life Photographing Hollywood's Most Famous*, is a memoir of those years. C'mon. Admit it. Every time you're in the line at Safeway, you can't keep your eyes off the tabloids. The only thing that's holding you back is the fear that one of your friends is going to see you with your nose in it reading about the latest breakup of Brad and Angie, the newest indignity of Lindsay Lohan, or what Kristen Stewart looks like in a bikini."

Boy, did I have fun working on this proposal. The story is filled with Hollywood tittle-tattle. And there were lots of opportunities to lampoon the pretenses of celebrity culture, and throw in Jennifer's stunning tabloid photos just to make it pop. (I'll put the complete Overview of *Shooting Stars* at the end of this chapter. It's a hoot.)

Shooting Stars is, as I have said, a "high concept" book. She didn't have to spend much time describing it further. So Jennifer included some sly humor in that same paragraph because... well... how could she resist? It's always nice to have a little fun with a proposal when the opportunity allows. And acquisition editors, like the rest of us, need some laughs in their lives as well.

Now let's take a look at another quite different book. *Inferno: A Doctor's Ebola Story* by Dr. Steven Hatch, published by Saint Martin's Press in 2017. Steven is a professor of epidemiology at University of Massachusetts Medical School. As we mentioned above, in 2014 at the height of the Ebola epidemic, he volunteered to work at an Ebola treatment unit in rural Liberia. Steven and I had a number of long distance conversations about his idea for this book while he was in Liberia, in the course of which we traded a lot of gallows humor. *The New York Times* helped us out by publishing a rare front page feature along with color images (nytimes.com/2014/10/17/ world / africa/ ebola-liberia-west-africa-epidemic.html). The main doctor being profiled was Steven. People still remember the heartbreaking photo of Steven dressed in a space suit holding a dying child in his arms. Of course we put that picture on the cover of the book proposal; and when I sent the proposal around to publishers, all of them remembered the story.

> "Inferno is a physician's memoir of the Ebola outbreak in Liberia. It describes the life of an Ebola Treatment Unit at the height of the epidemic in October 2014, when patients were felled by the hundreds each week and families and whole communities were torn apart at the seams. It documents the ravages of the disease, produced by an invisible particle one billionth the size of the human body that it so efficiently destroys. And it takes stock of the human response, both from within West Africa and from without, providing a first-person perspective on the public health implications of the outbreak."

After the first two paragraphs of The Overview, you need to move on and give the editor a better sense of what the book is about. I always ask my clients to describe some features in the text that are unusually dramatic or otherwise attention grabbing. Some of my proposals even do it in bullet points. This is the chance to work your magic, to show the editor why this book is important, why readers (and the media) will get excited about it, and why you are the best person to be writing it. The remainder of The Overview might be as short as two double spaced pages (that's usually too short) and as long as nine.

Below are several complete Overview texts by some of my clients:

Shooting Stars: My Unexpected Life Photographing Hollywood's Most Famous, by Jennifer Buhl.

Note: This Overview was fun to write and is fun to read, but it required considerable thought. Jennifer's book is filled with adrenaline packed action, lots of gossip, some hysterical schlemiel type humor, but it also has something honest and important to say about the role of celebrity culture in America. We tried to balance both those messages. Jennifer even came up with an inspired pitch line: She described the book as: "Indiana Jones meets Bridget Jones." Most of all, we wanted to give it a real sense of fun, drama, and glamour. I think we succeeded. So did Hollywood. *Shooting Stars* was optioned and put into development for a scripted series with a major network.

Check out the "hook" at the beginning of The Overview. It's also the beginning of the book, so it has a quadruple impact. It lets the editor know exactly how the story starts; it's a scene with an attention grabbing celebrity; There's action; and it's funny.

My lunch shift at Tropicalia, the Brazilian restaurant up the street from my apartment, has just ended. I'm sitting on the restaurant's patio drinking coffee and reading the newspaper. I didn't come to L.A. to be a waitress, but I'm thankful for the job. I hear the brakes and look up. Eight blacked-out SUVs have come to a screeching halt in front of White Trash Charms, the boutique across the street. I watch as seven guys jump out of their vehicles and a beautiful, skinny blonde gets out of hers. It could be a mugging or robbery, or possibly gang violence.

No. It's Paris Hilton. Shopping.

I've never seen paparazzi in action. For ten minutes, the guys press their cameras against the store window, bursts of flash going off every few seconds. When a meter maid walks up to write Paris's car a ticket, one of the paparazzi tries to negotiate on her behalf. Unsuccessful, he instead captures the ticket-writing moment. When Paris exits, the men crouch in front of her, moving backward while taking her picture. It's very physical, but somehow oddly friendly.

Paris leaves in her Escalade, followed by a chain of similarly sized SUVs. I notice one nice-looking Latino paparazzo has stayed behind and is sorting through pictures on his camera. I amble over and strike up a conversation with the first question that comes to mind: "How much do you make on a picture?"

"Oh, at least five hundred," he says.

Holy Snap. Right then and there, it's like God whacks me over the head. I have fifty dollars in my pocket and less in my bank account. My life is lackluster and I want more. I just haven't figured out how to make "more" happen.

"Do y'all ever hire girls?"

Thus begins my three-year career as a paparazza. *Shooting Stars: My Unexpected Life Photographing Hollywood's Most Famous* is a memoir of those years. C'mon. Admit it. Every time you're in the line at Safeway, you can't keep your eyes off the tabloids. The only thing that's holding you back is the fear that one of your friends is going to see you with your nose in it reading about the latest breakup of Brad and Angie, the newest indignity of Lindsay Lohan, or what Kristen Stewart looks like in a bikini.

Rest assured, you can read some of that in my book—there is juice. And non-stop action. I stake out celebrities for a living! Backs of cars. Tops of trees. Undercover in hotels and restaurants. But ratting on celebrities was never my purpose in writing this book, and *Shooting Stars* doesn't read like one long tabloid article. It's not about celebrity scandal either. Rather, it is a personal story that brings to life the breathless world of paparazzi—the real people behind the cameras—and the surprisingly complicated relationship between the photographers and the stars. It is a vulnerable story, too, with heartache and love and the tick-tock of a biological clock (mine, that is). It's a little like Indiana Jones meets Bridget Jones.

All of us have read the sensational stories of blood-sucking paparazzi—how they chased Princess Diana to her death, and more recently how they invaded the privacy of Kate Middleton's holiday to photograph her sunbathing topless. Remember the Britney Spears underwear-less shot?—now we've got a new one of Anne Hathaway, snapped sans undies as she was exiting her car at the New York premier of Les Miserable.

Who are these vultures behind the shots?

For three years in Los Angeles, I was one. I probably don't fit into your image of a paparazzi. For one thing I'm a woman, a mom. I'm not rude or particularly manipulative. I get embarrassed. My feelings got hurt when celebrities would get angry at me. And while I would never have sold a picture of a woman's private parts, I did follow some celebrities at high rates of speed. Usually I was smarter than that, but sometimes adrenaline clouded my judgment. Like it does the celebs, especially the young ones.

The public doesn't hear our side of the story very often. Mostly we are quiet. We don't like to be interviewed. We hide behind our cameras. Our pictures are ubiquitous though, and our names are printed in magazines and blogs around the world. Our "artwork" is devoured—women and men, college graduates, high school dropouts, high earners, low earners, Americans, Italians, Brits and Norwegians, everyone sees it. It's you who Google the images of Britney and Brad and Taylor and Kim, and you who scour the blogs to see what the stars are wearing, how they've done their hair, who their boyfriends are, and what they look like in bikinis... or without underwear.

Celebrities need exposure. Many of them cultivate relationships with "paps" (that's our street name.) A lot of them have our cell phone numbers. Many tip us off about where they will be and when, dressed up, posing... begging for a photo. Some of them (like the Kardashians) even get paid a percentage of their photo sales. In spite of what you hear, we aren't just chasing them. A lot of stars work us as much as we work them. Paris Hilton was the master of this. Nobody else even came close. There are, of course, the ones who don't like to get photographed. It's almost impossible to get pictures of Cameron Diaz, Leonardo DiCaprio, and Jennifer Aniston, for instance. I did, though.

I try to capture it all in this book. It's personal. It's all in my voice, and it's about my direct experiences. Some examples:

My fears when I'm careening down Melrose going through red lights trying to catch up with Zac Efron.

Being busted on a film set while secretly photographing Nicole Kidman and getting humiliated by her husband, Keith Urban.

The most awkward two minutes of my life stuck in an elevator with Cameron Diaz.

Gotcha!! A photograph of Kristen Stewart smoking pot on the week of the release of Twilight.

How I got pushed around by a douche bag pap trying to keep me from getting in his way. I bit him in the hand. He sued me.

How I fell for Aaron, a paparazzi... and Adrian, a celebrity.

I incorporate the colorful pap vocabulary into the story—kind of Tom Wolfe-like. When the paps surround the star like a wolf pack, we call it "gangbanging." When we stake out a star, waiting patiently in front of her house (or in her bushes) all day or even all week, we call it "doorstepping," and we call the target "the doorstep." There's even a pap dictionary in the back of the book.

What might surprise you is that in spite of the unflattering pictures and the scandals you read about in the Safeway line, we really like to get positive pictures. That's what the tabloids pay for—stars looking gorgeous. Fashionable clothes, pregnancy glows, boyfriend kisses, bikini beaches.

I bar no holds with pap secrets. I have included some really fun information boxes in sort of a "paparazzi-ing for dummies" way, and you'll find several "lists:" the 5 tips a celebrity needs to know when trying to avoid the paps; the best cars to drive if you're a celebrity who doesn't want to be spotted (including a list of what the stars actually drive); and the tools you need to set up your own "pap kit." I even have an extremely tacky star map of West L.A., which unlike the ones you buy on Sunset Boulevard actually has good information. I also had "a thing" of leaving notes in celebrities' mailboxes with tips for them, too—some well received, others not. (Hence, the little restraining order threat by Kate Bosworth.)

I finally gave up my career as a pap when I had a baby (though I worked when I was pregnant, and that's all included). Having a family was always more important than the adrenaline rush of my job, it was just how to get there. I was pretty successful though. In a profession of almost no women, I earned a lot of respect from the men. At the height of my career, I was bringing home about $10,000 a month and publishing profusely every week. That put me in the top 5% of paparazzi earnings.

I try to portray the celebrity life and the pap life as it really is. And I think you will see very clearly how glamour isn't always that glamorous. The stars are just trying to live their lives, and regardless of whether they are pap friendly or pap averse, most of them are good people. (Well, maybe not Kate Bitchworth, excuse me, Bosworth.)

The action is non-stop. And the stars are all here: David Beckham, Britney Spears, Jessica Alba, Matthew McConaughey, Jennifer Aniston, Miley Cyrus, Halle Berry, the Olsen twins. And more and more and more. The same ones you read about at Safeway.

America is obsessed with celebrity. It permeates media and dominates our thoughts. The paparazzi, while unseen, are at the center of the culture of celebrity and are its keenest observers as well as critical participants in the process. And while we see and read about the stars everywhere, don't you sometimes wonder if you really know them? Celebrity is as ineffable as it is pervasive. I'd like to believe that by reading my book, you will get a better understanding of what it's all about—and what's actually behind the beautiful faces.

As I read the text of this again now, I'm struck by the authenticity of Jennifer's voice. We all strive in our writing for a "natural voice." It isn't all that easy to achieve. A book like this could easily have degenerated into snark, which would have made it sound supercilious and unappealing. "Voice" is ineffable, but it's critical to good writing. Make sure you think about this when you are writing your own Overview.

Here's the complete Overview of *Inferno: A Doctor's Ebola Story* by Steven Hatch. It's one of the shortest Overviews I have worked on. We avoided listing all the dramatic scenes. We felt it might have sounded too grim. But also we didn't really know too much about what the book would be like. Steven had written the draft of this in Liberia under harrowing conditions risking his life every day treating the victims of the contagion and watching so many of them dying.

What we did know was that he was a good writer. (He'd been a journalist before going to medical school.) And we wanted to find a publisher before all the other Ebola projects would start floating around New York. In spite of the short length, I think it works pretty well. It's clear that the story is going to be dramatic but also break away from a purely personal narrative. We supplemented this text with pictures by *New York Times* photographer David Berehulak showing Steven at work in the treatment center. No words could describe that experience any more eloquently than those pictures.

Inferno is a physician's memoir of the Ebola outbreak in Liberia. It describes the life of an Ebola

Treatment Unit at the height of the epidemic in October 2014, when patients were felled by the hundreds each week and families and whole communities were torn apart at the seams. It documents the ravages of the disease, produced by an invisible particle one billionth the size of the human body that it so efficiently destroys. And it takes stock of the human response, both from within West Africa and from without, providing a first-person perspective on the public health implications of the outbreak.

It is my story. I am an Infectious Disease physician and an assistant professor of medicine at the University of Massachusetts Medical Center. I first came to Liberia in November 2013, before the outbreak started, to work at a hospital in Monrovia. I came to know and admire many of the physicians I worked with. A little more than six months later several of those doctors were dead or just clinging to life, infected with a virus that had never been seen before in that part of Africa. By July and August 2014, there was chaos on the streets of Monrovia, Liberia's capital city. I was watching the news reports with increasing alarm, knowing the fragility of the medical infrastructure of this country that had just recovered from a brutal and prolonged civil war. When I got the news that one physician whom I greatly regarded had died from Ebola, I resolved to go there to do what I could do.

I was not entirely sure I would live through the experience.

But I did, and as an Ebola doctor in rural Liberia from October through early November of that year, I bore witness to unimaginable suffering. I also did the things that doctors do and have done for generations, which is take care of patients to the best of my abilities. This book is, in large part, about those experiences.

However, it is also a story of the virus itself—an

explanation of the science and the biology of Ebola and the kinds of havoc it can wreak at the level of a nation, a family, a body, or a single cell. As much a book of popular science as a "pure" narrative memoir, Inferno tries to teach its audience about this disease through a doctor's eyes—as well as through those of nurses and social workers, my colleagues who also tended to Ebola's destruction of the body and the soul.

Finally, it is a story of the patients and their families torn apart by the Ebola crisis. The victims included the young, the old, and everyone in between; they included mothers who were negative for the disease and were separated from their children who were positive; they included patients who turned out not to have Ebola at all, but were held in "Suspect Wards" with patients who did have Ebola while they all waited for blood tests to return, sometimes for days, intermingling with one another. But there is a story of triumph here as well, as survivors volunteered to re-enter the treatment unit in order to care for loved ones, or found their calling in life and vowed to become a nurse or doctor or social worker and make helping others their reason for existence.

As I write these words in February 2015, I am sitting at a table in the very Ebola Treatment Unit where this near-apocalypse took place. Now, however, there is quiet. The staff—about one third the size of the operation from only a few months ago—look for small tasks to busy themselves. There hasn't been a patient with confirmed Ebola in more than 40 days. The crisis has abated, although that is not quite the end of the story. Ebola is not completely gone, and until the very last case has been tracked down, the country and the region are at risk of having this start all over again. The memoir approaches the end by considering this delicate moment in the history of Liberia and its neighbors that were also affected, Sierra Leone and Guinea. Lastly, I conclude by noting what my involvement has done to how I view medicine, and how I live my life.

I'm particularly proud of Mary Jo McConahay's *Tango War: The Allies and the Axis in Latin America:1935-1945*. It's almost impossible finding a subject associated with World War II that hasn't been extensively written about. Well, Mary Jo did it. The story of a whole theatre of the war that has never been covered. It's mostly a spy war, and a war for the hearts and minds of an entire region. This gave us some good opportunities to spice up the story. Of course, everybody loves to read about Nazis. But also America kept sending celebrities to Latin America for propaganda purposes. It's a serious work of history, but you will see people like: Nelson Rockefeller, Walt Disney, Carmen Miranda, Rita Hayworth, and Orson Wells weaving in and out of the narrative. The book is being published by Saint Martin's Press. Publication is scheduled for 2018. As I said above, titles are extremely important for marketing, and this one is fantastic.

Mary Jo is a legendary war correspondent. She covered the civil wars in Latin America during the eighties. One of the things we wanted to emphasize was the extent of serious original research that was going into this book. Maybe it was overkill, but the last paragraph shows the extensive research that Mary Jo is engaging in.

Tango War tells the suspenseful story of the secret race between the Allies and the Axis to secure the allegiance and natural resources of the Latin American continent before and during the Second World War. The narrative begins in the mid-1930s, when Nazis held the upper hand. Memorable characters, heroic and nefarious, carried out the struggle. The Latin-American Tango War, in which each side closely shadowed the other's steps, weighed heavily in the ultimate Allied victory in World War II. This book shows in a new way—with its Latin American locus—how WWII was truly a global war.

This book will:

- Explain the strategic importance of Latin America to the war effort of both sides

- Show the work of Nazi and Allied spies, intelligence and counterespionage operations

- Illustrate the economic and political influence of German, Italian and Japanese ethnic communities in Latin America, and the war's effects on Latin Jews

- Describe Nazi penetration of the continent, and Nelson Rockefeller's forward-looking counter-offensive using Hollywood stars and media campaigns

- Reveal the abuses of the Allied economic Blacklist and the phenomenon of the Latin American detention camps

- Explain the critical role of the U.S. take-over of the Brazilian hump in the invasion of Sicily, and in the Allies' African and European campaigns

- Tell the compelling, little-known story of the Brazilian Expeditionary Force, the only Latin American contingent to fight alongside Allied forces in Europe

- Describe the Vatican's "ratlines" for fugitive war criminals, showing how they fed the creation of Cold War death squads in Latin America and the dirty wars of the 1970s and 1980s

A 1933 aerial transport map of South America shows German hegemony in the skies, with hundreds of crisscrossing lines representing commercial and passenger routes flown by German companies. As Hitler campaigned to capture Europe, Germany was Mexico's biggest trading partner, the leaders of Brazil and Argentina were unabashedly pro-fascist, and the Southern Hemisphere was dotted with important ethnic German, Italian and Japanese populations, who carried with them more loyalty for "homelands" than for the Latin countries where they lived. Latin Americans of all kinds admired the way Hitler, Franco and Mussolini were bringing a kind of order to countries across the sea that once seemed as disorganized as Latin countries were—fascism was attractive. Pro-Germany or "neutral" governments, and strong economic and military ties, made the Latin American continent favorable to the Axis. From the American southern hemisphere, *Tango War* throws a fresh, new light on the timeless story of World War II.

The narrative is factual, delivered in the mood of the time when the outcome of the war was not certain. I am a journalist who covered modern war in Latin America during the 1980s. My style is influenced by the narrative richness found in the work of historians Barbara Tuchman and Rick Atkinson, with a nod to the well-researched creation of atmosphere found in the novels of Phillip Kerr and Alan Furst.

In 1938 President Roosevelt charged a Joint Commission of the War Department to determine

where an Axis engagement threatening the United
States might be most likely to come from. The answer:
South America. Planners drew the southern limit of the
U.S. defense perimeter not on the U.S. border, but on
a line running from Peru in the west, through the hump
of Brazil that juts far into the Atlantic. Drawing the line
was the easy part.

In the next years, like partners in a high-stakes
tango, following each other closely, even intimately,
intelligence agents from both sides, diplomats, and
military officers worked in ways mundane, ingenious
and often deadly to secure Latin America. In a loosely
chronological fashion, *Tango War* shows how the
shadow fight unfolded sphere by sphere, such as in the
struggle over command of the skies, where German
dominion was finally overturned at the hands of
cunning American businessmen and a legendary British
spy. And at sea, from the first engagement of the Battle
of the Atlantic on the Plate River off Uruguay and
Argentina, to the high point of U-boat mastery of the
South Atlantic off Brazil, when U.S. Liberty Ships were
the target. *Tango War* describes the fight to capture raw
materials invaluable to the war machines of both sides—
rubber, oil and precious rarities such as industrial use
diamonds.

One of the most colorful chapters of the effort to
win Latin hearts and minds was the propaganda and
economic warfare campaign headed by Nelson
Rockefeller. The future U.S. Vice-President, then
young, handsome, with family business interests
throughout Latin America, set out on a crusade to
counteract the Nazi penetration on the continent that
was overseen by Reich Minister for Propaganda Joseph
Goebbels. Rockefeller's Office of the Coordinator of
Inter-American Affairs (CIAA,) created in 1940,
answered directly to Pres. Roosevelt. The CIAA

brought Hollywood stars to the region to impress crowds and hobnob with government officials, a seduction by celebrity unprecedented in world affairs, but which would become a staple of U.S. propaganda efforts in the Cold War. Walt Disney arrived as a goodwill ambassador, as did Rita Hayworth, Orson Welles, Douglas Fairbanks Jr., Bing Crosby, Errol Flynn and many others. At the same time, the economic warfare arm of the CIAA was collaborating with British Intelligence and FBI agents at U.S. embassies to capture and intern thousands of persons deemed friendly to the enemy.

A gigantic historical shift took place during the *Tango War* years when Washington, in a series of landmark hemispheric conferences and backroom deals, was forced to abandon traditional gunboat diplomacy, which had governed U.S. policy since the early 19th century. In its place, diplomats engineered regional alliances, to ensure Latin solidarity with the Allied cause. This was how the Good Neighbor Policy became concrete.

President Roosevelt, in personal visits to Brazil–the key country to U.S. strategy–promised money, military and industrial aid. As a result of a tenuous, intense dance of diplomacy led by Roosevelt confidante Sumner Welles, the United States was able to launch a military base construction campaign that became pivotal to Allied victory in the Battle of the Atlantic. The Latin bases were integral to the invasion of Sicily that began the assault on occupied Europe, which ultimately defeated Nazi Germany.

In another little known episode told here, the Brazilian Expeditionary Force, 25,000 strong, became the only Latin American fighting unit to participate in Europe in the Second World War. Beginning badly, losing battles and men, the story of the "Smoking

Cobras" ends valiantly on the Italian Gothic Line, with the Brazilians capturing 14,000 enemy soldiers and three generals, including the entire 148th division of the German Army.

During the war the Vatican, Argentina and Germany laid the groundwork of routes that would become the infamous "ratlines" that took war criminals to freedom in Mexico and South America. The same ratlines also helped move selected Nazis to the United States under protection of U.S. intelligence, and Jews to Palestine. The ultra-rightist war criminals who travelled the ratlines to Latin America not only escaped punishment. They helped to orchestrate right-wing terror campaigns, establish death squads and advise Latin autocrats in their dirty wars over the next four decades from El Salvador to Argentina, campaigns that backed U.S. Cold War policy and took thousands of lives. Thanks to the ratlines, fascist bloodletting and fanaticism did not stop in 1945, but crossed the seas to Latin America in ways that affect the region to the present day.

My understanding of war and its consequences is not abstract, but concrete. I witnessed killing first hand, and destruction of towns and villages, as a journalist covering the Latin American wars of the 1980s and 1990s. Renowned linguist and political analyst Noam Chomsky singled out my work in El Salvador as coming from "one of the few U.S. reporters to spend time in the zones under attack," while Nation columnist Alexander Cockburn pointed to my "fine reporting" at a time when most U.S. press ignored "indiscriminate bombing." I have covered war for thirty years. I see the long-lasting effects of war: I have been the recipient of an Hibakusha Fellowship in Japan, interviewing survivors of Hiroshima and Nagasaki, and in 2013 I covered the long and emotional trial of the first former head of state to be convicted of genocide by the courts of his own country, Guatemala's Gen. José Efraín Ríos Montt, a series for which I received the First Place Gold foreign reporting award from the 250-member Catholic Press Association of Canada and the United States. I have spent the last four years researching the 1935-1945 period of *Tango War*, reviewing published and unpublished material in English, Spanish, Portuguese, and Italian, original sources including diaries and family histories, and interviewing historians and witnesses. I have conducted research in the following archives and historical collections:…

Production Details

This is a simple section. You want to tell the publisher the estimated number of words, date of delivery, number of illustrations, and any other details that bear on production and design. If your book is a gift book or one that features unusual design or formatting, you will have to provide the publisher with some of this information. Maybe even a mockup of a page or some sample photographs. But publishers usually reserve the right to determine the design elements of the book. And don't forget. In most book contracts, the author is responsible for securing and paying for all permission clearances.

Word count is always an important issue. In publishing, we talk about word count rather than page count. And in the age of the Internet, readers' attention spans are limited. People ask me how many words a book should be. There is not a definitive answer for that. Books that are primarily text and are less than 50,000 words though are frequently considered too short. Publishers have to justify charging $25 for the book. So they are thinking about the "package." And books that are too long incur higher production costs which may force them to assign a suggested retail price that will drive away buyers.

You may ask how can you know what word count to use when you haven't written the book yet. That's a fair question. You simply have to estimate it. Publishers tend to be flexible if the text comes in reasonably close to the prediction. If you specify a 100,000-word book in the proposal and the word count comes in at 110,000, you probably won't have a problem. Recently though I delivered the final text of a book where we estimated in the proposal a word count of 100,000. When the author was done writing, the text was 190,000 words. This was very much a problem. Remember the estimated word count is included in the book contract. If the delivered manuscript is dramatically longer or shorter, it could be grounds for termination. And you would have to return your advance.

The Audience

Writers always have difficulty with this section. Frankly, I do too. One of the questions acquisition editors ask is: "Who is the audience for the book?" Often writers will overstate their position. If the book project is about women's health, you don't want to say the audience for the book is women concerned about their health. That's pretty much five billion people. And we can be certain most of them aren't going to buy the book. An audience is different from a demographic. We need to define the audience as the sub-group who have a compelling interest in the subject and who might be willing to put down $25 to purchase the book.

The best way to do this is by analyzing competitive titles. That's the next part of the proposal. And we will get to that. This section is usually either more general or more specific. If you are writing a self-help book, say a book about managing back pain—you probably do want to give some demographics. How many people are hospitalized for back pain every year? What are the sales for various back pain remedies? All of these people won't buy the book, but it is an indicator the book is addressing a real problem.

I once represented a project about work related injuries. It was a good book by an author who had excellent platform. Still I couldn't sell it. The book included advice on a wide range of medical problems associated with the workplace. Publishers told me a person with back problems wasn't interested in reading about repetitive stress injuries. In other words, we weren't able to define the audience.

The other approach to this section is to bombard the editor with quantitative data. You usually see this in business plans in more traditional businesses. This becomes a problem when your book is narrative or creative non-fiction. How do you quantify an audience for a personal memoir, like *The Liar's Club* by Marry

Karr, or for narrative history, like Mary Jo's *Tango War*, or a collection of essays? In those genres, it's pretty hard to define the audience. That's why the only useful tool for identifying the potential readership is by analyzing competitive titles.

Here's a good example of a description of the audience from *The Drone Age: How Drone Technology Will Change War and Peace*, by Michael Boyle to be published by Oxford University Press in 2019. Because this book is being published by a university press, we tried to emphasize it was written for a wider audience than for just the academics in his field. We also wanted to highlight the fact that it might be used as a course adoption.

> "This book will be written for a popular audience and will avoid scholarly jargon and inaccessible language. Footnotes or endnotes will be used but the text itself will be free of academic language that clutters the narrative. But the book also has the potential to be assigned in undergraduate and graduate courses in political science and international relations. This book will also have a substantial policy impact, as it could be assigned or taught in military and government training academies, as well as read by policymakers at many levels of government. The goal would be for this book to be an essential resource for those working inside and outside of government on issues like warfare, terrorism, complex emergencies, repression and new technology."

Jennifer Buhl's *Shooting Stars* takes a different approach. She relies almost entirely on quantitative data. She could do this because it was possible to define her potential audience with some specificity. So she re-searched the readership statistics of the major tabloids and Hollywood gossip media. And she came up with some pretty impressive numbers. Because there are no other books about paparazzi published and because there are so many books by and about movie stars, we decided we couldn't do a particularly convincing Competitive Analysis. So we simply added a few representative book titles into our audience analysis.

Shooting Stars is the first memoir written by a paparazzi. There are hundreds of books by and about celebrities. For a sense of the potential audience for this book, below you will find market reach and demographic information of selected U.S. celebrity media.

Print Media (in estimated readership per issue)

People 42,000,000

US Weekly 13,500,000

Star Magazine 10,200,000

The National Enquirer 3,000,000

In Touch 7,200,000

Online media (in unique views per month)

People.com 12,300,000

US Weekly.com 8,900,000

TMZ 12,600,000

PerezHilton 12,000,000

The readership of all of above media is 70+% women

Selected Book Titles with Bookscan sales figures

Angelina: An Unauthorized Biography, Andrew Mortan (St. Martins, 2010) BS cloth 33,131

Kardashian Konfidential, Kim Kardashian et al. (St. Martins, 2010) BS cloth 154,861

Stories I Only Tell Myself, Rob Lowe (Henry Holt, 2011) BS cloth and paper 140,000

Is Everyone Hanging Out Without *Me*, Mindy Kaling (Crown, 2010) BS cloth 115,251

Most Talkative: Stories From the Front Lines of Pop Culture (Henry Holt, 2012) BS, cloth 42,458

Mommywood, Tori Spelling (Gallery Books, 2009) BS, cloth and paper 137,000

Competitive Analysis

The Competitive Analysis is probably the most important section for publishers attempting to determine the potential audience for your book. In this section publishers expect you to list five or six "competitive" titles, evaluate their strengths and weaknesses, and explain how your book differs. Many authors tell me there is no other book like theirs being published. This isn't a good pitch. When I hear this, it raises the reasonable question of why isn't there one. And the answer is usually that there isn't an audience for the subject.

What you ideally want is to show there are other books directed toward the same readers as yours and have sold very well. This indicates to a publisher there is a big potential audience for your book. So when you are preparing your list of competitive titles, it's best to find successful books, usually those published by major presses. If possible, avoid books published by small specialty publishers unless the book is the leading title in its class. Never use self-published books. Be careful about scholarly or technical books with very high list prices. This usually indicates the competing book is limited to a narrow audience.

Another mistake authors make is to find competitive titles and attack them mercilessly to convince the editor the competition is weak. You don't want to do this either. Remember my advice is to strive for transparency and honesty. You want to give an objective assessment of competitive books. Explain their weaknesses but also their strengths.

That disgusting fascist, Ezra Pound, coined the slogan for modernism: "Make it new." That should be your watchword too. If you have a good idea, there are in all likelihood other books on the same subject. You need to "make it new". Show how you are adding something that is significant, something that would induce a buyer to get yet another book on this general topic. Let's say you are an historian writing a history on the presidency of Thomas Jefferson. This would be a challenge. There are hundreds of books written about every aspect of Jefferson's life and work. If you are a Jefferson scholar, you might imagine, for instance, you have discovered a new facet of his relationship to his Secretary of the Treasury, Albert Gallatin. Although this may be a stunning discovery to academic historians, it isn't likely to be important to the general reader.

Not long ago I was attempting to sell a new book

about menopause. The author and I worked hard on the proposal to show the work she had done was original and different from other research in the field. And it was. We assumed the editors who looked at the proposal would recognize the importance and originality of my author's book. But most of them rejected it and simply commented that they didn't need another book on menopause. In other words, they didn't go very deep in analyzing our argument for the uniqueness of the project. To them, it was simply a marketing decision. Too many books on the same subject. One editor dismissed the proposal and just said "it was a well-tilled field."

In the modern world of publishing, acquisition decisions often get made by the numbers. And publishers have access to sales figures for almost every book in print by subscribing to the Neilson Bookscan point of sale data base. When publishers look at your book proposal, they will check the sales numbers for each competitive title on Bookscan. There is a fair amount of sales that don't get picked up by Bookscan, but it's the best indicator publishers have. If your Competitive Analysis includes 4 books on a given subject, all of which have shown modest sales on Bookscan, this will make it much less likely that they will want to acquire your project.

They will also look at any previous book you have had published in the same genre. If your track record was unimpressive, it's going to influence their decision to acquire your new project.

When I am working with authors on their book proposal, I always try to incorporate Bookscan sales numbers in the Competitive Analysis (particularly if the sales are impressive). You probably don't have access to Bookscan unless you have a friend working in publishing. In order to use Bookscan, you need to purchase an expensive license for a year. Many people include Amazon rankings in their Competitive Analysis. This isn't particularly useful. There are very few books that sell consistently year after year. Typically books sell well for some months. Then sales rankings decrease precipitously. If the comp book you are analyzing has a ranking of #1,000,000 on Amazon, that is an indicator of modest sales during the current period. (Very modest. Almost no sales at all.) But that doesn't mean it wasn't a successful book. It may very well have been a best seller at one time, but sales have dropped off.

Here's the Competitive Analysis from the proposal for *No Simple Highway: A Cultural History of The Grateful Dead* by Peter Richardson, published by St. Martin's Press. This project has the advantage of being about a subject with a vast and highly motivated audience. Dead Heads are the most fanatical fans in all of popular music. The challenge is that there were already a number of books on The Dead, and we would have to make our case distinguishing this one. The book was published in 2015 to coincide with the 50th anniversary of the band. But this was a mixed blessing. There were other books also published on the subject at close to the same time. In some cases, reviewers chose to feature one of these other books instead of Peter's. Additionally Dead fans weren't likely to buy every new book that was out. In other words, we had a lot of competition.

Peter listed eight books in his Competitive Analysis. That's more than most. At the beginning Peter introduces the section with an analytical paragraph describing how his project differs from the others. He also points out his book is the first to benefit from the material available in the newly opened Grateful Dead Archives. Peter did an excellent job of giving an impartial analysis of the competitive books. His format is pretty standard. Each book has its own paragraph and includes the author, the publisher and the publication date. Also note that he has Bookscan numbers. The sales for these competitive titles range from over 70,000 copies in cloth and paperback (very impressive) to about 3000 (not very impressive). Bookscan retrieves the point of sale information from all of the major book chains and most independents as well as Amazon. It doesn't have access to sales for e-books, library sales, big box stores, and other non-bookstore outlets. Check out Peter's voice. It's crisp and professional. Publishers like that. It sends the message that the author is realistic. Here's his comp analysis:

Many books have told the Grateful Dead's story, several in great detail, but none has combined a concise narrative with a perceptive account of the band's unique appeal. *No Simple Highway* builds on the rich insights of these earlier books as well as new archival material at UC Santa Cruz to fashion a compelling cultural history.

Note: Bookscan figures below do not reflect pre-2001 sales.

Phil Lesh, *Searching for the Sound: My Life with the Grateful Dead* (Little, Brown, 2005). Bookscan: Cloth,

46,015; Paperback 14,177. An appealing, valuable, well received, but inevitably partial account of the Dead's experience by its bassist.

Dennis McNally, *A Long Strange Trip: The Inside History of the Grateful Dead* (Broadway Books, 2002). Bookscan: Cloth, 45,794; Paper 29,536. The "official" history of the Dead, this 700-page volume is a treasure trove of information. McNally, who served as the band's publicist and holds a Ph.D. in American history, delivers the inside story promised in the subtitle. The sheer detail and enormous cast of characters complicate the narrative, and McNally's connection to the band weakened the book's authority for some reviewers. Even so, this is the standard.

Steve Parish, *Home Before Daylight: My Life on the Road with the Grateful Dead* (2003). Bookscan: Cloth, 9,769; Paper, 4,304. Garcia's key roadie reflects on the crew's rowdy hedonism, Garcia's connection to the Hells Angels, and his attraction to "weird America." Not a direct competitor.

Blair Jackson, *Garcia: An American Life* (Viking, 1999; paperback 2000). Bookscan: Paper, 28,876. Offers a detailed account of the band's history with special attention to its leader. The editor of a Dead fanzine, Jackson captures Garcia's passions, personality, and demons, but there's relatively little cultural context or analysis. Like McNally, he sometimes empties his note-book, especially on set lists and Garcia's drug use. Pre-Bookscan publication date.

Rock Scully & David Dalton, *Living with the Dead: Twenty Years on the Bus with Garcia and the Grateful Dead* (Little, Brown, 1996; paperback 2001). Bookscan: Paper, 8,148. A high-spirited romp co-authored by the band's manager and a Rolling Stone writer. Narrated in the first person and present tense, Living with the Dead is colorful but by no means a complete or especially accurate history. Pre-Bookscan publication date.

Carol Brightman, *Sweet Chaos: The Grateful Dead's American Adventure* (Clarkson Potter, 1998; paperback 1999). Bookscan: Paper, 5,064. An intelligent but idiosyncratic account of the band's place in American cultural history by the sister of the band's lighting director. Shifting between the band's history and her contemporary experiences in political journalism, Brightman offers many insights but saddles the Dead with a political overlay that was never part of their project. Pre-Bookscan publication date.

Peter Conners, *Growing Up Dead: The Hallucinated Confessions of a Teenage Deadhead* (De Capo, 2009). Bookscan: Paper 5,308. Explores the Dead's appeal from 1985 to 1995 from the perspective of a suburban teenager. Not a direct competitor to No Simple Highway, but shows the sustained demand for Dead lit, even from the groundling's view.

Robert Greenfield, *Dark Star: An Oral Biography of Jerry Garcia* (William Morrow, 1996; paperback 2009). Bookscan: Paper 2,958. Edited transcripts from 67 interviews conducted with Garcia's colleagues, friends, and family. Published the year after Garcia's death, Dark Star forgoes cohesive narration but captures the sensibility of the band's inner circle and offers many insights into Garcia's background and personality.

Here's another. *Blood in the Fields: Ten Years Inside California's Nuestra Familia Gang* by Julia Reynolds. Published by Chicago Review Press, 2014. This is a work of journalism about America's most violent Latino gang. The author, Julie Reynolds, has been a reporter for *The Monterey County Herald* and has been covering the gang activities for years. She also co-produced a documentary film on the subject. She begins the analysis with a paragraph explaining the uniqueness of her book. And like Peter Richardson, she is careful to describe the strengths and weaknesses of competitive titles accurately and objectively.

Many nonfiction books with a great story to tell about criminal and street subcultures have found wide reading audiences. None of these outstanding titles, however, tackle the Nuestra Familia gang and most of them take place in inner cities, whereas *Blood in the Fields* surprises readers both with its rural American setting and proximity to the jet-set glamour of the Monterey Peninsula. What the best of these have in common with is their engaging use of narrative to draw readers into the human drama at the root of every criminal empire.

Gang Leader for a Day: A Rogue Sociologist Takes to the Streets [Bookscan–hb: 74,056. pb: 25,728]

by Sudhir Venkatesh

Penguin Press (January 2008,) Penguin (December, 2008)

This *New York Times* bestseller has been described as "The Wire meets the University of Illinois." Venkatesh takes readers along for the often frightening ride as he immerses himself in the life of an urban gang for seven years. This bookish grad student's own struggle to overcome his fear of the young people he is trying to study is something readers can relate to so well they even feel his exhilaration at ultimately being appointed the gang's "leader for a day." The book has been hailed by Newsweek as a compelling text that "gives readers a window into a way of life that few Americans understand."

The Snakehead: An Epic Tale of the Chinatown Underworld and the American Dream [Bookscan–hb:3857. pb:5351]

by Patrick Radden Keefe

Doubleday (July 2009); Anchor (July, 2010)

The Snakehead grew out of a 2006 article for *The New Yorker* magazine, and is a sweeping portrait of an underground economy behind the twelve million undocumented immigrants living in America. Written by journalist Keefe, this richly researched tale is based on hundreds of interviews and government documents, and like, the plot swirls around a massive federal court case. Keefe's narrative tells the story of immigrant smuggler Sister Ping, but also digs into the lives of the gangsters around her and the FBI and immigration agents who pursue her. As a saga of the American dream, *The Snakehead* looks at the peasants who risk everything to take harrowing ocean crossings to America. Like *Blood in the Fields, The Snakehead* is deeply researched yet intimate, illuminating the broader issues that affect our society through a riveting narrative. The book was chosen as one of the best of 2009 by *Publishers Weekly, The Washington Post* and *The Chicago Tribune*.

Always Running: La Vida Loca: Gang Days in L.A.

by Luis J. Rodriguez

Curbstone Press (1993); Touchstone (2005)

This memoir by Rodriguez is powerful in part because it's presented as a true story he wrote to deter his own son from gangs. The reader joins Rodriguez in his beautifully told metamorphosis from likeable barrio kid to soldier willing to kill strangers for his gang's honor. In places it lacks the level of detail about specific crimes and events that I include in *Blood in the Fields*— in Rodriguez's case, the vagueness is understandable given the self-incriminating nature of his story. The book is very popular with schools, has been translated into Spanish and reprinted in a recent new edition.

The Black Hand: The Bloody Rise and Redemption of "Boxer" Enriquez, a Mexican Mob Killer [Bookscan–hb: 23,935. pb: 22,610. mm: 14502

by Chris Blatchford

William Morrow (2008); Harper Paperbacks (Sept. 2009)

Like *Blood in the Fields* this is a book by an investigative reporter who spent years researching his topic and had inside access to the Mexican Mafia, the Nuestra Familia's rival. Telling the tale of the rise and fall of one man who left the gang, this authorized biography received a starred review in Publishers Weekly and has been called "astonishing" and "groundbreaking."

Random Family: Love, Drugs, Trouble, and Coming of Age in the Bronx

by Adrian Nicole LeBlanc

Flamingo (Oct. 2003); Scribner Paperback (Jan. 2004)

As in *Blood in the Fields*, LeBlanc spent many years following the lives of her subjects. In more than 400 pages of tight, simple prose, she tells the epic story of several families in the Bronx and their struggles with love, street and domestic violence, and imprisonment. *Random Family* was named one of the ten best books of the year by *The New York Times Book Review*; it won the Anisfield-Wolf Book Award and was a finalist for the National Book Critics Circle Award.

Like *Blood in the Fields*, the book is strongly narrative, without journalistic interpretation and without insertion of the author into the story. Like *Blood in the Fields*, it has a cast of characters who would not be considered traditional heroes—and yet readers find themselves rooting for several of them all the way to the end. *Blood in the Fields* of course has its surprising rural Western setting, but also differs in that it occasionally steps back from the characters' immediate world to take the longer view of history, the perspectives of law enforcement and political leaders, and the story's place in America's wars on gangs and drugs.

Marketing and Promotion

In this section of the proposal you will lay out your plans for marketing your book. Most authors are utterly flummoxed by the idea of having to engage in marketing. I can see why. Writers are writers. They have chosen a solitary vocation. They aren't salesmen, aren't product marketers, aren't press agents or publicists, and usually not particularly good at self-promotion. But when your book gets published, you are going to have to assume the functions of all of these jobs. You need to put away that literary tweed jacket, stop walking around clutching your slender volume of verse, and start flogging your product. "It slices. It dices!"

Hey (you might be asking), isn't that what my publisher is supposed to do? If I have to do that kind of heavy lifting, why shouldn't I just self-publish it myself and get 50-70% royalties instead of 15%? Good question. And I probably don't have a very satisfying answer.

Certainly, self-publishing is an option. That's what I did with this book, after all. And publishing it was pretty easy. The e-book took about 8 hours. (This doesn't include the time I spent writing it. That took three months. And learning what I needed to know to write it took about 40 years.) It didn't cost much either. I had to pay someone $100 to design the cover. And I set the price: $3.99 for the e-book. I get about $3.00 royalty. Not bad. The paperback version was a little more complicated. But not that much. I had to pay someone to design and format the interior of the book, the front cover, back cover, and the spine. My total cost for preparation of the book was about $500.00. Then I sent it on to Ingram Spark, a service that specializes in printing and distributing print on paper books for self-published authors. Spark charges about $5.50 per book for production and distribution of a book of this length. It's available through Spark's parent company, the distributor Ingram Book Company, to all the bookstores and libraries of the world. I only make about $1.50 when I sell it to a bookstore through Spark but I get about $6.00 when I sell direct. If the book was published by a traditional commercial publisher, I would get 90 cents for each copy in paperback and $1.50 for each e-book.

A lot of self-published authors contact me and ask if I will try to find a commercial publisher for their self-published book. They almost always tell me they want the marketing power of a traditional publisher to take the book to the next level. Well... not to deliver bad news... ok... here's the bad news. Almost every author I have ever spoken to has been cruelly disappointed by the efforts of the publisher in promoting his book. Publishers do have marketing budgets, but most of that money goes to their "A list" titles. You will be assigned a publicist, but she will likely have 12 other books she is working on simultaneously. She has a great rolodex and will send out press releases and review copies to an impressive list of media contacts and reviewers. But she doesn't have much control over who will respond. The number of review venues has declined precipitously since media has migrated to the Internet. TV is great, but it's very much celebrity driven. Talk radio is probably the best venue for promotion. But again, there is lots of competition for a limited number of slots.

Of course, you can always hire a freelance book publicist to supplement the work of the publisher. And sometimes that makes a lot of sense. Here's what independent book publicist, Mary Bisbee Beek says about the additional marketing a freelance publicist can offer:

> "Publishers believe that most of the PR and marketing for a book takes place four to six months prior to the launch date. If by the launch date you don't have a number of reviews lined up, three to four solid readings in bookstores or private venues that make sense, social media, and a myriad of other details; then the ride down the slippery slope starts early. But if you engage with an independent publicist for at least half of the time that the publisher's publicist is working on the book and for three or so months after the book launches, you will have the benefit of an extra set of eyes, hands, and years more experience and extra contacts. The more that you do, the more books you will sell and the louder your voice in social media will be. In short, an independent publicist can help get you more reviews, additional event outreach, additional word of mouth, a new and possibly more creative perspective, all adding up to additional publicity beyond launch

date. And don't forget social media and Internet marketing. Last, but not least, what's the best form of
social media? Word-of-mouth! Find a publicist that you
like, that you respect and trust, and you'll have a much
better time!"

Mary is an outstanding book publicist. If you are
trying to decide whether to hire one either for your
self-published or traditionally published book, you
should definitely check out Mary (www.marybisbee
beek.com).

Now let's talk about the Internet. The Big Enchila-
da. The elephant in the publicity room. There's good
news and there's bad news about the Internet. The
good news is much of it is free. The bad news is most
publishers don't seem to know how to promote online,
and aren't inclined to put out the energy to do it. That
leaves you, gentle reader. The Internet is chaotic and
time consuming, but you have to do it. Marketing gurus will tell you to blog, tweet, get involved in social
media, put up a book or author website, have a
Facebook page, ferret out possible blogs for blog interviews, and take a "blog tour." Some of it won't work.
But some of it will, and the benefits are cumulative.

In the end, I can't tell you whether you should
choose self publishing or traditional publishing. When I
first became an agent in 2008, it seemed like all the
tech gurus were saying that traditional publishing was
dead. It was a dinosaur that couldn't adapt to the Brave
New World of the Internet. They liked to throw out
big words nobody really understood like
"disintermediation." Blah, blah, blah. It turns out self-
publishing is something of a mixed bag. Its weaknesses

are inherent in its virtues. It's true in this Brave New World, anyone can become a published author. But without the filtering system of traditional publishing, the self-published world of books is an ocean of mediocrity. Within this ocean, there are great books, to be sure. But identifying them is difficult. There are some big fish stories of authors who have sold millions of their self-published books. These examples are rare. Most self-published books sell in the low three figures.

But the same is true of traditionally published books. Most of them fail to make money. Many of them sell modestly. But there are some definite advantages to traditional publishing. It has considerable prestige, particularly if you are published by one of the elite imprints like Farrar, Straus, and Giroux or Alfred Knopf. Most reviewers will only review traditionally published books. Most literary awards are only open to traditionally published books. Most bookstores will only stock traditionally published books. There is a certain prestige to having a book traditionally published. It has gotten through a formidable filtering system. People with judgment, experience, and taste at many levels have given the book a vote of confidence. There is real value here, even if it doesn't result in vast riches.

And let's be honest for a moment. Have you ever been to one of those elite, snooty, literary cocktail parties? Who are the authors surrounded by the groupies, those cool, sophisticated, gorgeous editorial assistants with degrees from Brown in creative writing and now working at Knopf? Why the authors who have been published by traditional publishers, that's who. And who's standing alone, probably next to the food table scarfing down the shrimp cocktails? The genre science fiction or romance author who is raking in $20,000 a month selling his e-books on Amazon for $2.99. Who would you rather be?

But still if your book is going to find its audience, regardless of whether you are self-published or traditionally published, you have to be a savvy marketer, not just a brilliant writer. The marketing section of the book proposal will describe to the publisher your plan to market your book once it is published. Most of the plans that come to me from authors in their draft proposals aren't very good. They usually fall between the Scylla of being totally lame and the Charybdis of grandiosity. Earlier on we talked about some very bad pitches, many of them were imbued with delusions of grandeur. My favorite "bad" pitch was by a client of great importance in his field. He said he would agree to be interviewed by Terry Gross on *Fresh Air* (the best talk radio venue in America)–time permitting. Time permitting, indeed!

At the other end of the scale, I see marketing plans which tell the publisher the author will have a publication party at her mom's house and might contact a local bookseller to (try to) schedule an event. These pitches are pretty weak. They say to the publisher you are a rank amateur. You need to convince them you are going to be a savvy marketer. And then you actually have to be a savvy marketer.

Remember the marketing section is about what you are going to do. You don't have to advise the publisher about what they already know. You don't have to make a list for them of major national periodicals to send review copies to. Don't engage in wishful thinking. Don't mention Oprah. Don't mention *Fresh Air*. Don't mention *The Daily Show*. Don't mention *The New Yorker* unless you are sleeping with someone who works at *The New Yorker* or have concrete information proving you will be invited to these venues.

The marketing should be about what you WILL do. Don't talk about what you MIGHT do. In the mind of the acquisition editor, the word "might" generally means "probably not" or even "not a chance in hell." And while you are at it, avoid using the word, "try"—as in "I will try to get Malcolm Gladwell to give me a blurb."

A good marketing plan has to be robust, but it also has to be realistic and convincing. Speak with authority. Keep a professional tone. Convince the publisher you understand the importance of marketing, that you are committed to doing it, and that you are aware of the opportunities and the realistic limits that will exist for you.

Here are some points you should be thinking about when writing your plan.

- **Websites**. Publishers expect you to have a website for your book. So you should mention you intend to do it. Now if you already have a website with lots of fans and lots of unique views, then you have a compelling pitch and you should make it.

- **Blogs and social media**. Publishers like authors to blog And if you have impressive numbers of followers and viewers, let the publisher know. But many writers aren't going to do blogs. Maybe you don't have that kind of time. So don't promise one unless you are committed to it. Publishers also expect you to engage in social media like Facebook and maybe Twitter, so you should address that. And if you have an abundance of friends and followers in social media, then let the publisher know. They love big numbers.

- **Media appearances**. If you have strong connections with media and have a realistic chance of getting bookings, then mention that in the proposal. It helps if you have had previous appearances in those venues or if you have close relationships with people who can help you line them up. But again, don't engage in wishful thinking.

- **Blurbs**. Blurbs are good, but make sure you either already have the blurbs or have firm commitments. It's ok to say Malcolm Gladwell will blurb your book if he has agreed to do it. You don't have to make a list of celebrities you will "approach" for blurbs, although by all means, start thinking about that. You are going to have to do this after you get the contract. Cynical wags in book publishing call it "whoring for blurbs."

- **Speaking engagements**. If you do public speaking as part of your job or your platform, then talk about the venues where you will be speaking at the time of publication. You should probably limit this to major venues with significant audiences.

- **Book signings**. It's ok to say you will aggressively seek out book signings. But remember, publishers usually make the initial contact with the bookstores.

- **Book tours**. Publishers won't send you on a book tour unless you are a huge author. Some authors will go on a tour at their own expense. If you intend to do this, mention it in the proposal. Give the publisher a list of cities and tell them you will work with them to line up signings and media appearances in those cities. And don't forget to mention that you will do it at your own expense. Publishers really like that phrase: "at my own expense."

- **Book groups**. Offer to meet with book groups reading your book or to do Skype appearances. It's always a little tricky trying to ferret out these groups. If you have ways of doing it, let the publisher know. Publishers love informal book groups. The group members buy tons of books. Some publishers have marketing people devoted exclusively to these groups. You've probably seen the suggested discussion topics in the back of certain novels.

- **Press kits**. It's nice to put this in the marketing plan, because it shows you are savvy at promotion. Describe the press kit a little. And if you have creative ways to disseminate it, let the publisher know. Again remember not to tell the publisher how to do their job.

- **Other stuff**. You should try to think of other creative ways to promote the book that won't be done by the publisher. Do blog tours, giveaways, op-ed pieces. Hire your own publicist, but let the publisher know and make sure you will be working closely with the publisher on promotion. Remember, a publicist will charge you no less than $5,000 (and probably a whole lot more). And it doesn't always work.

- **Platform**. Platform is a subject unto itself. I have another blog post called "Platform is More than Just a Website and a Blog" (andyross-agency. wordpress.com/2011/07/29/platform-is-more-than-just-a-website-and-a-blog/) If you have a platform, make sure you leverage it for marketing the book and explain in detail how you plan to do that.

Take a look at the marketing section from the proposal for *Tango War* by Mary Jo McConahay. She exudes a tone of authority and self-confidence. She says what she WILL do, not what she MIGHT do. She lists authorities who WILL blurb the book. She doesn't say she will approach a famous person to inquire if they might be willing to maybe give her a blurb. She throws out some demographic information where appropriate, sending the message that she has done some serious homework. Also she had a previous book, *Maya Roads*. She describes the kind of promotion she did with that book and how she will do the same with *Tango War*.

As a veteran journalist, lecturer and teacher of writing, I am well placed with personal and professional contacts to promote *Tango War*. I will actively solicit appearances, reviews, give interviews and in every other way participate in advancing sales of the book, including social media, Twitter, and a new *Tango War* website where I shall begin a regular blog, with links from my long-standing GlobeWatch blog, well before the launch of the book. Besides my own personal networks and efforts, I intend to hire a professional publicist to assist distribution of news about *Tango War* and coordinate media attention and appearances.

Among colleagues who will blurb *Tango War* are *New Yorker* Staff Writer Jon Lee Anderson (*Che Guevara, A Revolutionary Life; The Fall of Baghdad*); Brown University visiting scholar and former *New York Times* reporter Stephen Kinzer (*The Brothers: John Foster Dulles, Allen Dulles and Their Secret World War; All the Shah's Men: An American Coup and the Roots of Middle East Terror*); Trinity College professor and author Francisco Goldman (*The Art of Political Murder; Say Her Name*); *New Yorker* Senior Editor Peter Canby (*The Heart of the Sky: Travels Among the Maya*); Pulitzer Prize-winning ProPublica reporter Jacob Bernstein (*Vice: Dick Cheney and the Hijacking of the American Presidency*, with Lou Dubose);... Besides traditional channels, I will also promote *Tango War* in the travel book and touring market, where it can answer demand for a solid and entertaining history of the growing travel destination of Latin America. The United Nations World Tourism organization recorded 27 million inbound arrivals in the region in 2013, and projects that number to reach 40 million by 2020. Brazil just hosted the FIFA World Cup, while the International Olympic Committee, for instance, expects some 480,000 tourists will descend on Rio de Janiero alone for the 2016 Olympic and Paralympic Games.

I participated fully in launching and promoting my previous books: *Maya Roads, One Woman's Journey Among the People of the Rainforest* (Chicago Review Press,) winner of the Northern California Best Creative Nonfiction Book and several other literary awards;... Reviewers called *Maya Roads* "brilliant," "a gift of rare courage and insight," and "an extraordinary literary journey," and I appeared promoting the book at venues across the country, which I will do with *Tango War*. I will market *Tango War* not only at targeted venues such as WWII and American history clubs such as the O.S.S. Society, for instance, and the David Rockefeller Center (Harvard) for Latin American Studies, but widely, such as I did with Maya Roads. Here for instance is a partial list of venues where I read from and lectured on Maya Roads, places I expect to appear with *Tango War*: [Mary Jo provides a long list of venues]. I will also spread the word about *Tango War* through my teaching and reporting network. I am on the faculty of the well-attended annual San Miguel de Allende Writers' Conference, give writing workshops for the global Eat-Travel-Write group, and belong to the San Francisco Writers Grotto, the Bay Area's oldest and most prestigious writing center, where I also give classes. I am a contributing editor for NewAmericaMedia.com, and write regularly for the oldest U.S. Catholic weekly, *The National Catholic Reporter*...

This is Julie Reynolds' marketing plan for *Blood in the Fields*. As with Mary Jo above, Julie speaks with an authoritative voice.

To put it immodestly, as a person considered by law enforcement, gang members, and fellow reporters to be the nation's top journalist expert on the Nuestra Familia, I pretty much own this topic. As such, I regularly appear before audiences at readings, speaking engagements, conference panels, university classes, hospitals, churches, and film screenings, where I have a ready platform ideal for promoting the book around the country.

My plan is to aggressively push this existing platform upward. I will increase the number of personal appearances, produce and book online live interviews and talk shows and promote the book through existing Twitter, Facebook, and YouTube accounts. (My documentaries on YouTube have received more than 1 million views.) I'll schedule interviews and features in mainstream news media, where I am fortunate to have many personal contacts. Because I am a former graphic and web designer and documentary producer, I am eager to produce an interactive web site with shorts videos, background biographies and photographs of characters, and add updates about the lives of those featured in Blood in the Fields.

I expect the book to draw interest from the many communities vexed by gang and drug problems, which broadens the book's natural appeal from the West to Eastern and Midwestern cities, and increasingly, rural areas in states such as Virginia that are seeing gang violence for the first time. I will tour for readings and take part in panels and forums in these communities, again reaching out to contacts in the media, publishing, and academia.

I have been interviewed many times about gang issues and my past investigations on KQED-TV, NPR member stations, Univision-TV (national), numerous local news affiliates of CBS, NBC and ABC-TV; and by *The Los Angeles Times*, *The San Jose Mercury News*, *The New York Times* and *The Nation*, and I will approach those outlets to talk about *Blood in the Fields*. I am an active member of several national journalists' associations and have received interest from many top reporters about covering the topic and my book when it is published. Several of my former Nieman classmates from Harvard are feature writers and pop culture critics at major U.S. newspapers and NPR, and have asked me to let them know as soon as the book has a publisher.

I will contribute related op-ed pieces to daily newspapers, NPR stations, and prominent websites, as well as my own sites, JuliaReynolds. com and NuestraFamiliaOurFamily.com.

I am fluent in Spanish and well-connected with ethnic media in the United States. I'll reach out to Spanish-language television, newspapers and radio, which I am sure will be eager to bring the book's themes to their audience of millions, many of whom are bilingual, English-language readers. (A future Spanish translation of the book would also find a welcome market with this audience.)

I will promote the book to teachers and librarians through online channels already used to disseminate my PBS documentary about the Nuestra Familia. The Center for Investigative Reporting has developed a very well-received teachers' guide and curriculum that helped sell the DVD to libraries, colleges, and high schools and led to a second printing. I have already begun promoting the work at readings and engagements booked this year for Monterey Peninsula College and the Monterey Institute of International Studies, where I am currently a fellow researching the roles of women in gangs. Staff at the David Rockefeller Center for Latin American Studies at Harvard assure me I am invited to speak anytime at their Cambridge, Mass, campus, where in the past I have read excerpts from the book-in-progress.

Book club coordinators at San José State University with City of San José public libraries have already told me they plan to include the book among their annual book club selections as soon as it is published.

About the Author

This section gives you the opportunity to present your credentials for writing the book and your ability to promote it when it is published. That, in a word, is "platform." As in all parts of your proposal, you want to be honest, transparent, and businesslike. But at the same time, you will need to shed your native modesty and be willing to make a compelling argument that, well, you are great!

Let's face it. Some people just don't have much platform at all. Although this is a disadvantage, you are going to have to rise to the challenge. You probably don't want to be so honest as to say: "Gee, I really don't have much of a platform. But I still have a really good book." People who write memoirs often say: "I am the ultimate authority on this subject. After all, the book is about me." This isn't a particularly good pitch either.

Most people have some kind of platform. Well...

Not always. Sometimes I get proposals by retired insurance salesmen from Frankfurt, Kentucky who are putting forth their opinions on how to end gridlock in Washington. But they are the exception. Here's a list of points you should consider addressing in this section.

What are my credentials as a writer? Have I been previously published? Have I written shorter journalism pieces? Have I won awards for my writing? Have I studied writing in a Master of Fine Arts program? Have I worked with an established writer?

What are my credentials in the field that I am writing about? What is my experience working with the subject of my book? Have I given classes on the subject? Have I given speeches at major venues? Have I written articles? What kind of recognition have I received from my peers? Have I won awards?

Have I published books on the same or different subjects? How did they sell? Did I get reviews or blurbs? [You should have a separate sub-section of blurb and review quotes. Don't use Amazon reader quotes. They are not considered reliable and they often come from friends and family. There is also a brisk business selling services writing five-star reviews for Amazon, usually for $5-$10 a pop.]

Have I been featured in periodicals, TV, Internet sites, or radio discussing this or other subjects? [You might want to include copies of some of these article in the appendix section.]

Below are two examples of the "About the Author" section written by my clients, Michele Anna Jordan and Mary Jo McConahay. As you can see, these authors have impressive platforms that include a large number of previous publications, awards, and peer recognition. Their authority shows they have a clear understanding of the elements of book promotion. Many of you will have less impressive platforms, but you need to present yourself in the best possible way and to make a convincing case for your authority and your ability to promote your book. But at the same time, remember my iron clad rule that you must be honest and transparent.

This is the "About the Author" section from the proposal for *More Than Meatballs!: From Arancini to Zuccini Fritters and Everything Inbetween* by Michele Anna Jordan. This is an excellent section Michele composed. It certainly didn't hurt that she has experience and platform. There are a number of points Michele wanted to make here. She needed to establish her credentials as a food expert, as a food journalist, as a cookbook writer, and as a person who is media savvy. Michele has extensive publication credits and has been nominated and won many awards including the prestigious James Beard Award. I've known Michele for about 40 years. But when I read this, I was still pretty impressed.

> Michele Anna Jordan is a second-generation Californian who has lived in the San Francisco Bay Area her entire life. During her twelve years as a chef she received numerous awards, yet in the early 1990s, she shifted her professional focus to her first love, writing.
>
> Michele Anna Jordan's first book, *A Cook's Tour of Sonoma*, enjoyed wide critical acclaim for its celebration of the agricultural bounty of Sonoma County. Published in 1990, the book was the first publication to acknowledge what the rest of the country has only

recently come to realize, that Sonoma County is one of the richest, most diverse agricultural regions in the world. In 2000, Jordan published *The New Cook's Tour of Sonoma* with 150 new recipes, an in-depth look at Sonoma viticulture, and an exploration of both the region's history and future. In 2002, Jordan completed a series of short documentaries about Sonoma's viticultural areas that aired on PBS stations throughout the country.

Jordan's writing is shaped by a distinct, lyrical voice. For ten years, "The Jaded Palate," a first-person narrative, appeared weekly in Sonoma County newspapers. Currently, she writes three weekly columns for the *The Santa Rosa Press Democrat*, "Seasonal Pantry," "Wine of the Week Food Pairing" and "Mouthful." Jordan is a regular contributor to *Savor Magazine*, which recently took a first place award from the Association of Food and Wine Journalists and has received numerous other awards since its launch in 2002. Jordan's essays appear in anthologies, such as the *Travelers' Tales* series and *Saltwater Sweetwater*, a collection of fiction and nonfiction by women writers from the north coast of California.

Jordan's first five books were published by Addison-Wesley Publishing Co. When *The Good Cook's Book of Tomatoes*, one of four books in her Good Cook's series, was released in the spring of 1995, the late Jim Wood of *The San Francisco Examiner* declared, it "easily one of the best food books I've seen in five years." Her ninth book, *California Home Cooking* (Harvard Common Press,) was voted Best Cookbook in the 1998 Small Press Awards.

In the fall of 1995, Jordan launched "Mouthful: The Wine County's Most Delicious Hour" on KRCB-FM (www.micheleannajordan.com/mouthful.html). Mouthful was a James Beard Broadcast Journalism

Award nominee in 1998, 2003, 2004 and 2008.

In 1995, Jordan joined *San Francisco Focus Magazine* [now *San Francisco Magazine*] as restaurant critic and contributing editor. She also worked as the North Bay restaurant critic for the *San Francisco Chronicle*. Jordan has written for numerous national publications, including *Cooking Light*, *Wine Enthusiast*, *Kitchen Garden*, *Fine Cooking*, *Bon Appetit*, *Food & Wine*, *Asian Week*, *Appellation*, *Sky*, *Wine & Spirits*, the *Electronic Gourmet Guide*, *food.com*, and *Au Juice, The Journal of Eatin', Drinkin',* and *Screwin' Around*.

Jordan teaches and lectures on a variety of topics including salt, pepper, pasta, polenta, mustard, olive oil, California olive oil, writing, the farm-restaurant connection, and more, and is a frequent guest on radio and television around the country. In the fall of 1998, Jordan was a featured speaker at the annual Pepper and Spice Seminar in Kuching, capital of Sarawak, one of two Malaysian states on the island of Borneo. In 2003, Jordan choreographed the production of The World's Biggest BLT©, a 106-foot-long sandwich. In 2007, Jordan beat her own record with a 130-foot-long BLT.

Michele lives in western Sonoma County with her two black cats, Poe and Rosemary, three Apple computers and a 1954 Seeburg Select-o-matic-100 jukebox. In 2002, she returned to one of her first loves, dance. She now studies and occasionally performs traditional Hawaiian hula and is at work on several new books, including a literary memoir about love, loss and hula.

—Books

Vinaigrettes and Other Dressings. Harvard Common Press, 2013

Travelers' Tales: The World is a Kitchen. ed. O'Reilly, October, 2006.

Veg Out! Gibbs Smith, Summer, 2004.

The BLT Cookbook. Morrow, Spring, 2003.

The New Cook's Tour of Sonoma. Sasquatch Books, Fall, 2000.

[Michele continues with a long list of books going back to 1990]

—Collections & Anthologies

Travelers' Tales Provence. O'Reilly & Associates, Inc., 2003.

Holiday Celebrations. Cooking Club of America, Fall, 2002.

It's All About Dessert. Cooking Club of America, Spring, 2001.

Something New! The Ethnic Entertaining Cookbook. Cooking Club of America, Fall, 2001.

—Awards, Nominations, & Appointments

2008. James Beard Foundation: James Beard Media Awards for Radio; Nominee

2004. James Beard Foundation: James Beard Electronic Journalism for Radio; Nominee.

2003. James Beard Foundation: James Beard Electronic Journalism for Radio; Nominee.

2002. Friend of Sonoma County Agriculture Annual Award. Sonoma County Harvest Fair.

1998. Best Cookbook (California Home Cooking) Small Press Book Awards.

—Selected Appearances

Today, NBC TV, June 1, 2003.

"Perspectives," KQED-FM.

"Food Nation with Bobby Flay," TVFN, Spring, 2002.

Mollie Katzen's Show, PBS, 2000.

Chef for Winemaker Dinner at the James Beard House, New York City, October, 2000

"Forum" with Michael Krasny, KQED, Fall 1999

Here's the About the Author section in the proposal for *Maya Roads: One Woman's Journey Among the People of the Rain Forest* by Mary Jo McConahay. Mary Jo is a legendary journalist who has been covering stories about Central America for 30 years. She was a fearless war correspondent during the insurgencies in the eighties. Although she was well known by her peers, she wasn't a household name. One of the goals we had in this proposal was to show how much Mary Jo was admired–even revered–by other prominent war correspondents and commentators. I think we succeeded. We played to her strength and began the section with quotes about her from prominent journalists. The section is considerably longer. I have abridged it.

Mary Jo McConahay was one of the most perceptive journalists working in Central America. She possesses a keen eye, a passionate sense of empathy, and an irresistible writing style. Those who either watched her work or read her dispatches will be thrilled to learn that she has turned her considerable talents to a memoir."

–Stephen Kinzer, former New York Times correspondent

"I have known and admired Mary Jo McConahay

for more than a quarter century, since we were colleagues at Pacific News Service in San Francisco. We both alternated between spells on the desk and long road trips to Latin America and Asia in those years. That gave me an opportunity to edit her brilliant work, which in truth seldom needed any editing. There are very few reporters with her ability to make a story come to life–to carry us so deeply into the struggles of the people and places she describes that we are nearly participants. This is journalism at its profound best, not a dry, detached exercise in analysis, but a plunge into the very heart of the human condition."

–Frank Viviano, former correspondent-at-large at the *San Francisco Chronicle*, is a commentator for CBS5.com.

Mary Jo McConahay has been a journalist for over 25 years. Her work has appeared in more than thirty magazines and periodicals, including *Vogue, Rolling Stone* and *Time* (see publications "At a Glance" attached,) and collected in half a dozen books, such as *El Salvador in the New Cold War* (Grove) and *True to Life Adventure Stories by Women*, Vols. 1 and 2, (Diana Press). She is a true traveler–more than 60 countries–who worked as a model and flight attendant before becoming a full-time writer.

The author began her professional career freelancing in Mexico; her first staff job came in the late 1970s at the *Arab News*, the largest English language daily in the Gulf region, when she was based in Al Khobar, Saudi Arabia. In the 1980s and 1990s, she covered the Central American insurgencies as an independent correspondent for the *San Francisco Chronicle* and *Examiner*, *National Catholic Reporter*, as Latin America editor for *Pacific News Service*, wrote for New York *Newsday* and other newspapers, and for periodicals including the *Los Angeles Times Magazine*.

During that time she also traveled to Poland, Brazil and throughout Central America for the United Nations quarterly, *Choices*, writing on human rights and development issues. Recently, she wrote a series of cover stories for *The Texas Observer* on the border wall and the border's militarization (*"Everyone talks about the militarization of the border, but few write about it like MARY JO McCONAHAY"*—*U.S.C. Annenberg Institute for Justice and Journalism, 2006*). The Society of Professional Journalists' Jon Marshall noted McConahay's border coverage in 2007 on the respected blog, *News Gems, Highlighting the Best of American Journalism*. Her writing, he said, stood in the tradition of the *Observer's* "journalism legends such as Willie Morris and Molly Ivins.

In 2000, McConahay's meeting with a troubled Iowa mother who had been a Maya war orphan led to writing front-page stories for the *San Francisco Chronicle* and the *National Catholic Reporter*, and co-producing the prize-winning PBS documentary, *Discovering Dominga*.

An amazing film, poignant and powerful.

–Elizabeth Farnsworth, The NewsHour with Jim Lehrer

This moving and very human film makes the recent history of Central America, especially Guatemala, come alive...

–Beatriz Manz, Prof. of Geography and Ethnic Studies, University of California, Berkeley

Discovering Dominga has won the Cine Golden Eagle Masters Award; the Best Documentary Award at the Los Angeles Latino International Film Festival; the Bermuda International Film Festival Best Documentary; Hollywood's Imagen Foundation Film Festival Best Documentary, and other honors; it has been an official selection in more than thirty-five national and international film festivals.

When two of McConahay's short stories appeared in a landmark 1980s anthology, *True to Life Adventure Stories by Women*, Alice Walker cited "...the wonderful 'Tehuantepec,'" and critic Francine Krasno called McConahay the "best of what is new and valuable in feminist fiction."

No one... has ever done a better job of capturing what it feels like to have bullets—American bullets—aimed at ending your life... She slogs through the same media world as the rest of us, but with an endless insistence on the new angle—on the deeper story behind the story—that redeems our profession.

—Media Alliance ceremony presenting award to McConahay

The *National Catholic Reporter* nominated McConahay for the Pulitzer Prize for reporting on the War Against the Church in El Salvador, 1990. In recognition of the practice of describing the human face of historical events, she received a Hibakusha Peace Fellowship in Hiroshima and Nagasaki. Alexander Cockburn and Noam Chomsky have highlighted her work in published writings.

The author graduated (B.A., English) from the University of California, Berkeley. She lives in San Francisco with her husband, a ceramicist, and their college-student daughter.

McConahay's major feature stories in *Vogue* (1992) and *Los Angeles Times Magazine* (1990) brought more reader response than any run to their dates, according to editors. "Global Warning" (*Vogue*) examined the pattern of the global heterosexual spread of AIDS. "Baby Trade" (*Los Angeles Times Magazine*) described the emotional complexity of foreign adoptions, for birth mothers and adopting mothers. McConahay exposed the illegal process of providing infants for foreigners in Honduras, leading to termination of corrupt steps in the process.

For *Newsweek*, for which she was a stringer, McConahay obtained the first interview with Rigoberta Menchu, the Guatemalan Maya indigenous activist, when Menchu was named Nobel Peace Laureate, 1992.

McConahay also has reported on abuses in the so-called war against drugs. In *Mother Jones* (1986) McConahay and co-author Robin Kirk published an investigative report on the U.S. drug war in Colombia and Peru which, they found, used glyphosate and an ingredient of napalm, dropped aerially for defoliation and eradication, including in the Amazon headwaters region. The story led to public attention, a congressional hearing, and to the Ely Lilly pharmaceutical company canceling a $25 million government contract.

Table of Contents and Chapter Outline

I usually combine the Table of Contents and the Chapter Outline of the proposal together. Some agents prefer them to be separate elements. Either way is ok. Since publishers are paying you a huge amount of money in advance for your project, they don't want to be sold a pig in a poke. (Actually, the above statement isn't entirely true. Most likely your advance will be insultingly small when compared to the amount of work that has gone into your book.)

But publishers do have a right to know what they are buying. You might reasonably ask how you can provide a complete and accurate outline of the book before it is written. Usually things change—mostly for the better—in the course of writing. Publishers know this, and good editors will even work with you to refine your concept and strengthen the book while you are writing it. More often than not though, they will wait until you submit your first complete draft and then provide you with editorial notes requesting changes. The chapter outline, at best, will give the editor a sense of the material you will be covering and the arc of the narrative.

Authors are often unsure how long their chapter descriptions should be. There is no set rule, except the descriptions need to be clear and—well—descriptive. Some authors choose to describe a chapter in a single paragraph. Others will take two pages. When in doubt, be as detailed as possible.

Writing the outline will be enormously helpful in your own efforts to come to grips with a strong organization of your book. A confusing chapter outline tells the acquisition editor the book might end up being unintelligible. One of the most frequent reasons for rejection I get from editors is "there isn't a strong 'narrative arc.'"

Below is the table of contents and chapter outline of *The Drone Age: How Drone Technology Will Change War and Peace* by Michael Boyle. This is relatively short and simple. Michael chose to provide a separate table of contents. And he has limited his chapter descriptions to a single paragraph. He didn't go into detail about the front matter. Although he doesn't have an "introduction" in the outline, it is clear from the description the first chapter serves as an introduction to the text.

We previously mentioned one of the purposes of the Chapter Outline is to indicate the narrative arc of the book. Narrative arc is usually a term associated with fiction and creative non-fiction. Novels, memoirs, narrative non-fiction books need to have this three act structure: a beginning, a middle, and an end. Michael's book is being published by Oxford University Press. It is a scholarly book. As such, narrative arc is less important. But he still had to struggle with creating a logical and intelligible organization to the book. I think he succeeded admirably here. The first chapter is an introduction where he lays out the different themes. It's followed by several chapters on the use of drones in warfare, both by nation states and by terrorist organizations. This is a subject we are all familiar with, at least superficially, from reading the news. He follows with an alarming chapter on drone surveillance and its threat to a free society. But drones can also be used for good. The next chapter discusses the humanitarian uses of drones. The seventh chapter describes how drones are being developed and used amongst the different nations of the world. And the final chapter is a discussion about the future and a summing up. It is a simple and elegant organization. Clarity is important in a book proposal.

Chapter 1: The Drone Age

The first chapter will introduce the major themes of the book and review the history of drone development and use from its earliest inception to the present day. It will begin with the U.S. funding of radio-controlled aircraft in 1914 and follow the evolution of the technology to the development of drone prototypes in World War II. It will show how reconnaissance demands during the Cold War built a substantial military-industrial infrastructure inside the United States that allowed it to take the lead in drone development in the late 1970s through the 1980s. It will follow this story through the use of drones in conflicts during the 1990s, such as Bosnia and Kosovo and the development of armed drones, which led to the decision to begin targeting individuals with drone strikes in 2002. Thematically, it locates the development of drones within wider revolutions in military affairs, emphasizing how advances in satellite technology and communications enabled the coming of the drone age.

Chapter 2: Automated Warfare

Chapter 2 will consider how drones are used in combat in Afghanistan, Iraq and elsewhere, providing a force multiplier for conventional military forces and providing new capabilities for precise targeting and even autonomous action by drones. Thematically, this chapter will situate the development of drones within the context of the Revolution in Military Affairs (RMA) that came to fruition during the Persian Gulf War. The rapid adaptation of new technology to combat, particularly the use of the Internet-based communication and satellite technology, constituted a significantly leap forward in the capabilities of the United States and other leading governments. This leap gave the U.S., UK and Israel an edge in defense production which allowed them to take advantage of drone technology in combat...

Chapter 3: Death From Above

This chapter will examine how drones have been increasingly used by the United States for targeted killing in Pakistan, Yemen and elsewhere. It will follow the development of the targeted killing program from its inception to the present day, focusing on the development of a bureaucratic infrastructure in CIA and the Joint Special Operations Command (JSOC) that allowed the Bush and Obama administrations to use targeted killings in an increasingly large number of countries. It will discuss and critique the Obama administration's arguments about the effectiveness of drones against al Qaeda and other terrorist groups, as well as the legal and moral dimensions of this practice. It will conclude by asking whether drones are creating a seductive illusion of bloodless warfare that will normalize this lethal practice in other countries. Interwoven among the descriptive elements of this chapter will be narratives of drone pilots, who are accused of acting as if they are playing a video game when killing others but in fact see the reality of killing in all its gruesome detail.

Chapter 4: Terrorist Drones

This chapter will review the so-far unsuccessful efforts by terrorist organizations to develop and use drones. It will trace the development of drones by Hamas and Hezbollah and show how each has deployed them to bait Israel to different results. It will examine al Qaeda's efforts to build and buy drones as an illustration of the technological limitations facing terrorist organizations that use drones, but contrast this experience with al Qaeda's effective portrayal of the damage cause by drones against the U.S. in its propaganda war. It will explore the growing tactical use of drones on the battlefield by the Islamic State in Syria. Finally, this chapter will look at opportunities and obstacles faced by terrorist organizations who want to use drones for attacks in the developed world. It will explore a number of scenarios for their misuse, including the risks of spreading radiation via widely available commercial drones, as occurred in Japan in April 2015.

Chapter 5: The All-Seeing Drone

The next chapter will examine the issue of surveillance, considering how democratic states have begun to use drones to monitor their borders and the activities of their citizens, while non-democratic states have turned to drones to detect, and sometimes, repress dissidents in their societies. It will begin by considering the use of unmanned spy drones by democracies for a range of surveillance activities, such as tracking criminals, illegal immigrants, and even environmental conservation. In the U.S., federal agencies (such as the Department of Homeland Security,) state and local law enforcement and even private organizations are all using drones to monitor legal and illegal activity. In the UK, for example, governmental authorities are now using drones to monitor reckless motorists, agricultural thieves and litterbugs...

Chapter 6: Disaster Drones

Chapter 6 will also examine the rise of "disaster drones," which now operate in complex humanitarian emergencies, such as natural disasters and civil wars. In these environments, surveillance drones have proven useful in crisis-mapping and search and rescue in natural disasters in Haiti and the Philippines, and more recently at the Fukushima nuclear crisis in Japan. Small surveillance drones are ideally suited for taking on the "dull, dirty and dangerous" jobs that are so needed in these situations. Drones have also been used during peacekeeping missions for aerial surveillance in missions in the Republic of Congo and Chad. In the future, disaster drones are predicted to be able to transport cargo and drop humanitarian aid in complex and dangerous environments (such as the Syrian civil war) in which humanitarian organizations are reluctant to send their own personnel. This chapter will also discuss some of the unease that NGOs feel over adopting drones, as these so-called "bots without borders" bring with them a host of logistical, political and moral obstacles.

Chapter 7: The Race for Drones

Chapter 7 will examine the global diffusion of drones across the world and consider the consequences of this shift for international peace and security. The global proliferation trends are striking: while the U.S. maintains a lead in the sophistication of its drones, it is no longer the leading exporter of drones, as both Israel and China have claimed a significant share of the export market. The diversification of the market will put drones in the hands of a wider range of state actors and even terrorist groups over the next several decades...

Chapter 8: The Future

The final chapter of the book will return to the theme of technological change and do some horizon-scanning for next-generation drone technology. It will look at the rise of autonomous and semi-autonomous drones, as well as the emergence of micro-drones which can be as small as a bird or an insect. It will discuss the exponential rate of technological change and adaptation and speculate how this change will transform war and peace in the 21st century. The book will conclude with a discussion of what options the United States has for managing global drones proliferation and setting new rules to govern their use in a world where almost everyone–friend or foe–has access to this technology.

Below is the outline of the book proposal for *Showstoppers!: The Surprising Backstage Stories of Broadway's Most Remarkable Songs* by Gerald Nachman. This is another book that is not a traditional narrative. So the organization is thematic. The outline conveys the message that this book is definitive, and the author has an encyclopedic understanding of his subject. It's also important to note the final text was considerably different in organization from what we laid out in the proposal. It was also considerably longer and precipitated some wrangling with the publisher. In the end, though, the publisher was happy with the result.

Table of Contents

Overture (Introduction): The roots of one musical theater fanatic's passion, secular religion and incurable disease–the personal journey that brought me from "The Mikado" at Oakland High School to cast albums, revues, Broadway and this book.

Not Just Another Openin' (show-stopping

openers–i.e., show-starters: "Tradition" (Fiddler on the Roof,) "Willkommen" (Cabaret,) "Old Man River" (Showboat,) "Heart" (Damn Yankees,) "I'm the Greatest Star" (Funny Girl,) "Something's Coming" (West Side Story,) "Oh, What a Beautiful Mornin'!" (Oklahoma!) etc. Aptly enough, the book opens with a chapter on landmark openers, songs that establish the mood and style of the show, tell audiences what to expect, set the scene and get things off to a rousing start. A shows can rise or fall on its opener. A great opener lifts a show into orbit instantly; a bland opener creates an uphill slog in Act 1.

Star Turns (songs fashioned for stars and songs that created stars): "Everything's Coming Up Roses" (Ethel Merman,) "Hello, Dolly!" (Carol Channing,) "Don't Rain on My Parade" (Barbra Streisand,) "I Cain't Say No" (Celeste Holm,) "Whatever Lola Wants" (Gwen Verdon,) etc. Stars inspire songwriters to craft a number for a performer's stage persona; many stars demand them. Or the right number sung by the right actor can make a star overnight, e.g. "Miss Marmelstein," the comedy number sung by Barbra Streisand in her first Broadway show, I Can Get It for You Wholesale, which critics so raved about that it sent her on her way.

Patter Songs "Why Can't the English?" (My Fair Lady,) "Trouble" (The Music Man,) "Nothing" (A Chorus Line,) "Brush Up Your Shakespeare" (Kiss Me, Kate,) "Anything You Can Do" (Annie Get Your Gun,) "Can-Can" (Can-Can,) "The Rain in Spain" (My Fair Lady,) "You're the Top" (Anything Goes,) etc. If anything separates show tunes from pop tunes, it's a patter song, always dependent on wit and wordplay (and lots of clever verses) to delight audiences, each verse a kind of reprise. Artfully crafted patter songs, like "You're the Top" or "Mr. Goldstone," virtually define the Broadway musical, with sharp verbal jokes and jabs, catchy rhymes and infectious melodies.

Heart-Stoppers–show-stopping ballads: "What's the Use of Wonderin'?" (Carousel,) "I Have Dreamed" (The King and I,) "People Will Say We're in Love" (Oklahoma!) "I Got Lost in His Arms" (Annie Get Your Gun,) "If Ever I Would Leave You" (Camelot,) "How Are Things in Glocca Mora?" (Finian's Rainbow,) "The Party's Over" (Bells Are Ringing,) etc. These silent show-stoppers are harder to determine because they don't elicit big applause, cheers and whoops of delight. They're the heartfelt songs that can choke you up or move you in quiet ways every bit as effectively as the big splashy show-stopping numbers.

Blockbusters–show-stopping chorus numbers: "Hello, Dolly!" (Hello, Dolly!) "Of Thee I Sing, Baby" (Of Thee I Sing,) "There Is Nothing Like a Dame" (South Pacific,) "Master of the House" (Les Miserables,) "If My Friends Could See Me Now" (Sweet Charity,) "Get Me to the Church on Time" (My Fair Lady,) "You Could Drive a Person Crazy" (Company,) "We're in the Money" (Forty-Second Street,) etc. These are the irresistible "take-home tunes"–the big slam-bang numbers, usually with scores of singers and dancers, meant to ingrain a show forever in your head (and in Broadway history,) one of the gut reasons that musicals still exist and survive.

Songs of Myself–highly introspective numbers, interior monologues: "I've Grown Accustomed to Her Face" (My Fair Lady,) "Where or When" (Babes in Arms,) "Soliloquy" (Carousel,) "I'm the Greatest Star"

(Funny Girl,) "Hymn to Him" (a k a "Why Can't a Woman Be More Like a Man?") (My Fair Lady,) "Why Was I Born?" (Sweet Adeline,) "I Could Have Danced All Night" (My Fair Lady,) "If I Were a Rich Man" (Fiddler on the Roof,) "Rose's Turn" (Gypsy,) "I'm Still Here" (Follies,) "A Puzzlement" (The King and I,) "Hey, There" (Pajama Game,) etc. Most solos are first-person songs but these numbers go well beyond that into ruminative, questioning, regretful or deeply tortured feelings.

Finales and "11 O'Clock Numbers": "I Don't Need Anything but You" ("Annie,")" "The Best of Times" ("La Cage aux Folles,") "Empty Chairs at Empty Tables" ("Les Miserables,") "You Gotta Have a Gimmick" ("Gypsy,) "Sit Down, You're Rockin' the Boat!" ("Guys and Dolls,") "Lullaby of Broadway" ("Forty-Second Street,") "Shall We Dance" ("The King and I,") "Forty-Second Street" ("Forty-Second Street,") etc. The big closer or close to the closing song (still called "11 o'clock numbers" from an era when curtains went up 8:30 or 9 and often ran past 11 pm). is designed to send you out of the show singing or humming. You may not have been dazzled by up till then, but these songs can get you to change your tune.

Appendix

The Twenty Greatest Showstoppers of All Time:

—"Trouble"
—"You're the Top"
—"Get Me to the Church on Time"
—"Hello, Dolly!"
—"Don't Rain on My Parade"
—"Cabaret"

—"There Is Nothing Like a Dame"
—"I Cain't Say No"
—"Anything Goes"
—"One Day More"
—"What I Did for Love"
—"If I Were a Rich Man"
—"The Impossible Dream"
—"I Am What I Am"
—"Adelaide's Lament"
—"Anything You Can Do"
—"Tomorrow"
—"Everything's Coming Up Roses"
—"We're in the Money"
—"America"

This is just a tentative list of possible numbers to discuss, from which the final choices will be made. Boldfaced titles indicate the excerpts included in this proposal packet.

Sample Chapters(s)

I won't include any writing samples from my clients' books. You are on your own with that. Writers always want to know how much they should include. I normally ask for at least one chapter or 25 pages. Some agents prefer 50. Authors also want to know whether they should always use the first chapter of the book. My answer is you should use the material that will most likely engage the acquisition editor. Sometimes it's the first chapter. Certainly publishers want to see how a book starts out. But often the first chapter is introductory. You may want to consider another part of your book.

Whatever parts of the text you decide to use, the writing needs to be strong and compelling. How you write is almost as important as what you write. This is certainly true of narrative non-fiction and memoir. But also true of every other genre as well.

Appendix

Every book proposal doesn't need an appendix, but you may have material that would otherwise disrupt the flow or organization of the proposal that might best be put in an appendix. Some examples are: a curriculum vitae of a scholar, magazine clippings, extended articles by or about the author, long reviews of previous publications, charts, photographs, or any other detailed or extensive material that would be of relevance to the proposal.

Now Get to Work!

If you have read this entire book, you now know as much as I do about how to write a great book proposal. You have already thought long and hard about the thesis or the central idea for the book, whether the book has something important to say that hasn't been said before, whether the book will have a wide audience that will interest a commercial publisher, whether you have the knowledge to write about it and the reputation to be taken seriously, and whether the organization and voice will be accessible to the audience you are trying to reach. Remember that even your best efforts may still not be rewarded with a book contract from a prestigious publisher. But you have to believe your book will change the world, so you need to just gird your loins and take the risk.

Book Proposals in this Book

All of the examples from proposals in this book were from projects I represented and were acquired by a book publisher.

Michael Boyle, *The Drone Age: How Drone Technology Will Change War and Peace*. Oxford University Press, 2017

Jennifer Buhl, *Shooting Stars: My Unexpected Life Photographing Hollywood's Most Famous*. Sourcebooks, 2014

David Dayen, *Chain of Title: How Three Ordinary Americans Uncovered Wall Street's Great Foreclosure Fraud*. New Press, 2016

Steven Hatch, *Inferno: A Doctor's Ebola Story*. Saint Martin's Press, 2017

Michele Anna Jordan, *More than Meatballs!: From Arancini to Zucchini fritters and Everything in Between*. Skyhorse Press, 2014

Mary Jo McConahay, *Tango War: The Allies and the Axis in Latin America—1935-1945*. Saint Martin's Press, 2017

Gerald Nachman, *Showstoppers!: The Surprising Backstage Stories of Broadway's Most Remarkable Songs*. Chicago Review Press, 2017

David Sedlak, *Water 4.0: The Past, Present, and Future of the World's Most Vital Resource*. Yale University Press, 2014.

Julia Reynolds, *Blood in the Fields: Ten Years Inside California's Nuestra Familia Gang*. Chicago Review Press, 2014

Peter Rudiak-Gould, *Surviving Paradise: One Year on a Disappearing Island*. Union Square Press, 2009.

About the Author

Andy Ross founded the Andy Ross Literary Agency in 2008. Prior to that, he was the owner of the legendary Cody's Books on Telegraph Avenue in Berkeley for 30 years. Andy represents authors in a wide range of genres. In non-fiction he particularly likes journalism, narrative non-fiction, popular science, history and current events, and books about society that tell a big story. In fiction, Andy represents authors of literary, commercial, middle grade, and teen fiction. In addition to the authors mentioned in this book, Andy's clients include Daniel Ellsberg, Jeffrey Moussaieff Masson, Daniel Boyarin, Elisa Kleven, Milton Viorst, Randall Platt, Tawni Waters, Leonard Shlain, Ralph Gleason, and Beth Hensperger.

Andy is also an editorial consultant for writers not represented by his agency. He specializes in reviewing and editing book proposals, query letters, publishing strategies, and contracts.

Andy's website for editorial consulting is www.andyrossagency.wix.com/andy-ross

Andy's agency website is www.andyrossagency.com.

Visit Andy's Blog "Ask the Agent" at www.andyross-agency.wordpress.com

CPSIA information can be obtained
at www.ICGtesting.com
Printed in the USA
BVHW040242290519
549396BV00015B/277/P